C Living and Working in Canada

A comprehensive and practical guide

If you want to know how...

Getting a Job Abroad
The international directory

How to Retire Abroad
Your complete guide to a fresh start in the sun

Living and Working in Spain
The complete guide to a successful short or long-term stay

Buying a Property in Spain
An insider guide to finding a home in the sun

Buy to Let in France
How to invest in French property for pleasure and profit

Please send for a free copy of the latest catalogue to:

howtobooks

Spring Hill House, Spring Hill Road, Begbroke,
Oxford OX5 1RX, United Kingdom
info@howtobooks.co.uk
www.howtobooks.co.uk

Living and Working in

Canada

A comprehensive and practical guide

3RD
REVISED AND UPDATED · THIRD EDITION ·

Benjamin A. Kranc
& Karina Roman

howto books

Published by How To Books Ltd,
Spring Hill House, Spring Hill Road,
Begbroke, Oxford OX5 1RX, United Kingdom.
Tel: (01865) 375794. Fax: (01865) 379162.
email: info@howtobooks.co.uk
http://www.howtobooks.co.uk

First edition 2000
Second edition 2002
Reprinted 2003
Reprinted 2004
Reprinted 2005
Third edition 2008

British Library Cataloguing in Publication Data
A catalogue record for this book is available from the British Library

ISBN: 978 1 84528 142 7

Cover design by Baseline Arts Ltd, Oxford
Produced for How To Books by Deer Park Productions, Tavistock
Typeset by PDQ Typesetting, Newcastle-under-Lyme, Staffs.
Printed and bound by Bell & Bain Ltd, Glasgow

NOTE: The material contained in this book is set out in good faith for general guidance
and no liability can be accepted for loss or expense incurred as a result of relying in
particular circumstances on statements made in the book. The laws and regulations are
complex and liable to change, and readers should check the current position with the
relevant authorities before making personal arrangements.

Contents

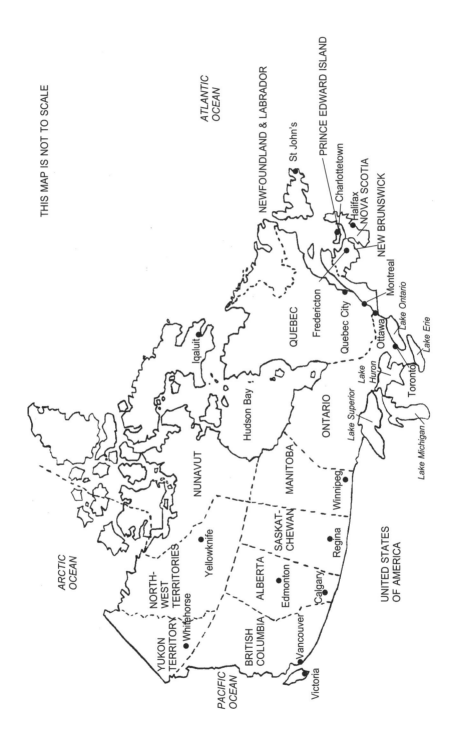

THIS MAP IS NOT TO SCALE

Preface

Welcome to the third edition of *Living and Working in Canada*. Canada is a very liveable country, something we're sure you'll agree with when you come yourself.

Whether your stay in Canada is to be permanent, as a temporary worker, as a student or as a holidaymaker, there is some fact and fiction to sort through before venturing to this huge nation. We hope that this book helps you to do so.

This edition has been fully updated to reflect the latest changes in how to get into Canada and enjoy living here. In addition to the ten chapters of information on what you need to know before coming to Canada, there is a useful address section at the back of the book. It is by no means an exhaustive list, but it should provide some good contacts to start with. Throughout the book and in the useful addresses section, we've included many more website addresses and email contacts than ever before.

Phone numbers in the book are listed with the city code in brackets followed by the phone number. Canada's international code is 1. All monetary sums are quoted in Canadian dollars, unless otherwise specified.

Much of the quantitative data in this book, the numbers that is, come from Statistics Canada, an agency of the federal government. Statistics Canada just completed its 2006 Census of the people of Canada. However, the agency releases the collected data to the public, on such things like population, religion and immigration slowly over the course of a number of years. We have used the latest data, when available, but in some cases we've had to rely on older statistics.

You may have heard alluring things about Canada from Canadians abroad who are missing home or from people from your own country who have visited Canada. Undoubtedly, you would have heard a bit about Canucks (an informal name for Canadians): that they don't mind the cold and are fairly laid-back. But relaxed as they may be about some things, they can get riled, becoming fervent about politics, especially when it comes to protecting their prized health-care and education systems, as well as the environment.

A century ago Sir Wilfred Laurier, Canada's eighth prime minister, said, 'The 20th century belongs to Canada'. In many respects, he was right. At the end of the last century Canada was rated number one out of 174 countries on the United Nations human development index, which takes into account life-expectancy, education and standard of living. It was the sixth consecutive year for Canada at the top of the list. However, in the last few years, Canada has fallen in the ratings to third and then to sixth place, after countries such as Norway and Sweden – a reminder that there's always room for improvement. Nevertheless, the new millennium promises to be as exciting as the last for Canada – something you will hopefully discover for yourself.

The adventure of going to a new country, for a short while or for the long term, can be a bit daunting. Just remember that under those bulky winter parkas, Canadians are a warm-hearted bunch.

We hope you have a terrific time in Canada and come to enjoy the country as much as we do. Best of luck.

The authors would like to acknowledge the help and support of many friends and family throughout the researching and writing of this book. Special thanks to Carole Whelan and Lynn Macdonald. Thanks also to all the front-line people in the various departments of the Canadian government for being so obliging with their assistance and advice.

Karina Roman and Benjamin Kranc
Toronto

① Deciding to Come to Canada

So you want to come to Canada, eh? First of all, contrary to widespread belief, we don't say 'eh' all the time. In fact, there are a few untruths out there about the country, one of which is that it's a cinch to get in. It's important to dispel the myth that Canada's doors are wide open to whoever wishes to enter, so that you can ensure you're one of those who does get in. Ninety per cent of skilled worker applicants are successful, but this is partly due to a preliminary self-assessment they are encouraged to do, resulting in many deciding not to apply. But, if you have the skills and the profile that Canada is looking for, you could be off to a new life in a vast and beautiful country. This book will help you to achieve your goals.

DEFINING YOUR GOALS

♦ Perhaps you want to come to a country less restricted and/or more stable than your own.

♦ Maybe you have family here whom you'd like to join, or you simply fancy a lifestyle change. You may feel Canada offers a higher standard of living than your own country.

♦ Are there employment opportunities in your field that don't exist in your country? Is there a business you'd like to start that you think would prosper better in a competitive and growing economy like that of Canada?

◆ Perhaps you prefer to first sample life in Canada through a working holiday programme or a limited-time working permit.

◆ Do you want to take a particular course of study at a Canadian university or college? Or are you just coming over on a short-term student exchange?

◆ Maybe you just want to backpack around the country or visit friends and relatives for longer than a few weeks.

KEEPING EXPECTATIONS REALISTIC

When you have determined your motives in wanting to come to Canada, it's important to identify the realities of what lies ahead. It's wonderful to have great expectations, but it's imperative that you become well-informed on certain aspects of Canadian life. There is plenty of opportunity, but no country is perfect.

Addressing myths and truths

Health care is free
What's that about there being no such thing as a free lunch? It's true in Canada that when you visit your family doctor you don't pay any money to the doctor directly. But the health care system is funded by the taxes Canadian residents pay. Canadian health spending is estimated to have reached almost 148 billion dollars in 2006. That's a little over $4,500 per person.

Multiculturalism has eliminated racism
Canada's **Multiculturalism Act** is indicative of a progressive society. Immigrants are 50 per cent more likely to be self-employed than other Canadians are and immigration accounts for 70 per cent of all labour force growth. In addition, they don't use

public services and social assistance as much. Despite these statistics there are people who believe that immigrants drain the welfare and social systems. Yet paradoxically, immigrants are sometimes accused of stealing jobs from long-time Canadians. Canada is known for egalitarian values and for being a 'cultural mosaic' rather than a 'melting pot', but that does not mean that racism is non-existent. However, in most cases Canadians know that Canada needs more people to continue to grow (the birth rate has been in decline for several years) and to prosper. In fact, in ten years' time it's estimated immigration could make up 90 per cent of the country's labour market growth and despite that, there are still predictions of labour shortages in some areas.

High-level skills lead to a high-level job
For the most part this is true. And the higher the level of skill and expertise you have, the better your chances of getting into Canada. For example, engineering, financial, science and health professionals score high points on immigration applications. Unfortunately, however, immigration does not take into account whether your certification or accreditation stands up in Canada. You could face years of further study in Canada – at your own expense – to be recognised in the profession you were in in your homeland. This challenge will be dealt with in the chapter on getting a job.

Seeing the up side
On the other hand, you may have heard a few discouraging things about Canada that are far from the truth, such as myths about bears in the streets, everyone living in igloos and it being cold all the time. In the following chapters you will learn more about Canada and, in turn, learn that the above is false. For example,

there is ready access to natural spaces where, yes, there are bears, but in the majority of cities the most aggressive wildlife you would encounter would be racoons ravaging garbage cans. Housing in Canada comes in all shapes and sizes and igloos exist only in the far north. In fact, with 90 per cent of Canada's population living 100 miles from the US border, most Canadians enjoy warm summers in addition to the cold winters – and in some parts of Canada, like the West Coast, the winters are actually quite mild.

JOINING YOUR FAMILY

One major attraction of moving to Canada may be that you have friends or family who have moved there already. Your relatives can help with advice and assistance in your application process. In fact, having immediate family can give you extra points on the application itself (the chapter on immigration deals with this). The adjustment to life in a new country can also be a great deal easier with the help of friends and relatives.

MAKING PREPARATIONS

Different preparations are involved depending on whether you are immigrating to Canada or coming on a student visa, a working permit or just as a visitor. For the purposes of this section, the following points mostly pertain to immigration.

Getting help
There are many people who do their own visa preparations when it comes to immigrating. Most buy a book like this one to get the information they need. Immigration Canada's website and local

consular offices also have detailed information on how to apply. But some people, especially those who feel they have complicated cases, might choose to hire an immigration lawyer or an immigration consultant. Both cost money, of course. Immigration lawyers are lawyers with a speciality in immigration and are regulated by their provincial law society. They will guide you through the process and try to minimise any legal quagmires that may arise. Immigration consultants are often less expensive than a lawyer and will guide you though the process, but they are not legal experts. It's also very important to note that immigration consultants are regulated by and must be in good standing with the Canadian Society of Consultants (CSIC).

Restrictions

Pets

It would be difficult to leave a beloved pet behind, but there are some conditions to be met in order to bring your animals with you. First of all, Canada is a signatory to international agreements banning the importation of exotic and endangered species. That means there are some animals you are entirely barred from bringing in.

But for those animals you can import, the conditions you must meet will depend on what type of animal you are bringing in and what country you come from, because some countries are certified rabies-free and some are not. Also, at the time of publication, birds from certain countries were banned from import because of fears of avian influenza (bird flu).

You will have to prove your animals are pets and that you don't plan to sell them. Depending on the animal and how old it is, there might be quarantine or vaccination requirements. For some animals, you'll need to get a permit to bring it in, which requires an application and a fee. Assistance dogs (seeing-eye, hearing-ear) are exempt from permit requirements if they accompany the person who needs the assistance.

Your pet will also be subject to an inspection when you come to Canada. You should also be aware that if you are coming to Canada temporarily, your pet may be required to be quarantined on your return to your home country, sometimes for long periods of time.

To find out what is specifically required for your pet, you can contact the Canadian Food Inspection Agency (CFIA) (see useful addresses). Their website (www.inspection.gc.ca) also has a wealth of information. CFIA also regulates the importation of plants.

Drugs

It's wise not to bring any drugs, except prescription drugs, into Canada. Even marijuana and hashish are considered narcotics and being caught with them carries a prison sentence. Can you think of a worse way to start your new life in Canada? You are allowed to bring in up to a three-month supply of prescription drugs as long as you can prove they were prescribed by a licensed physician and dispensed by a pharmacy.

Firearms

Canada has tight gun control laws. The federal law governing firearms is the **Firearms Act**. Individual provinces may have additional requirements, particularly regarding hunting. You must be 18 years of age or older to bring in firearms.

There are three classes of firearms: non-restricted (such as rifles and shotguns for hunting); restricted (for specific purposes such as target shooting, not allowed for hunting or self-protection); and prohibited. Prohibited firearms include automatic firearms and some semi-automatic ones, many handguns (depending on barrel length and calibre) and replica guns. They cannot be brought into Canada.

You must have a valid firearms licence and a Canadian registration certificate for each firearm. If you are coming just for a visit, you can declare your firearms through a non-resident firearm declaration (this must be signed by a customs officer at the border and is good for 60 days and the fee is $25) or apply for a five-year Possession and Acquisition Licence (PAL) and register your firearms in Canada. The latter option requires proof you have passed the required safety courses and costs $60 to $80 depending on the firearms.

If you are moving to Canada for an extended period of time or permanently, the PAL option plus registration is required. For more information, contact the Canada Firearms Centre (see useful addresses).

Health
Canada, of course, aims to prevent diseases from being imported into the country. You will need certain vaccinations for diseases. If you are immigrating you will have already been screened for diseases such as yellow fever and tuberculosis during your mandatory medical. If you are a visitor, a student or coming on a work permit, you may also require a medical depending on what country you are coming from or what occupation you may be

undertaking while in Canada (such as working with children).
Check with your Canadian Embassy or consulate.

STICKING TO YOUR DECISION

Once you start making serious preparations to come to Canada –
especially if it's to settle for good – you may begin to have
doubts. It is a courageous act to leave a life you know for one that
is unknown. You may be worrying about cultural differences,
homesickness or you may be afraid that your bravery will lead you
to failure. This is perfectly natural. Just remain clear about your
motives, informed about your choices and prepared for what will
greet you. And know that even if you don't have family or friends
awaiting you, you are not alone. There are agencies and
organisations in many Canadian communities that are set up to
help immigrants and new visitors.

Settlement

The host programme
This helps you get settled in your community. It is a free service
that introduces you to a Canadian who helps you learn about how
things are done in Canada. For example this person will help you
with the following:

◆ grocery shopping
◆ registering your children for school
◆ how to use local transport
◆ how to arrange television, phone and other utility services.

To join the host programme, contact a local immigrant service
agency (see Useful Addresses). There is also the Language

Instruction for Newcomers (LINC) programme and the
Immigration Settlement and Adaptation Program (ISAP).

Adjusting to culture shock

Canada is like most industrialised countries, so if you're from the
Western world you may not find it all that different. The greatest
adjustment will probably be getting used to the climate and the
vast spaces. Make sure the clothing you bring is appropriate for
the season, but don't overdo it. You don't need three featherdown
jackets all at once in the wintertime, but a warm jacket, gloves, a
hat and boots are necessary. If you bring clothing you can layer,
your wardrobe will be at its most versatile for any season.

Canada's biggest cities are so multicultural that anyone of any
race or religion is bound to find a community they can feel
comfortable in. Smaller towns, however, are less diverse and the
adjustment might be more dramatic.

Other than that, the differences are bound to be little ones only
you would notice: office etiquette, slang words, hours of operation
for businesses and shops etc. You'll soon settle right in.

Before you leave

If you're coming to live in Canada as a permanent resident, don't
sell your house or give up your job until your papers have come
through. You have about a year to get to Canada once you receive
your visa. Regardless of whether you're coming as an immigrant,
temporary worker, student or visitor, do not make any life-
altering decisions based on your travels, until you are certain you
are going and have your visa or work permit in your hand.

When you do come, don't pack your official documents in your suitcase, but carry them with you. This includes your passport; visa/immigrant papers for you and anyone else you are travelling with; birth certificate; baptismal certificates; marriage certificates; adoption, separation or divorce papers; school records, diplomas and degrees; trade or professional certificates; immunisation, vaccination, dental and other health records; driver's licence and any accident record from your insurance company; car registration (if you are importing your car); employer reference letters.

Also, bring with you two copies of a detailed list of all personal or household items you are bringing with you or that will follow you later. Last but certainly not least, make sure you have sufficient funds for short-term living expenses.

And off you go!

2

Learning a Bit About Canada

Canada doesn't often make the foreign pages of newspapers around the world. Many outsiders think of it as a snowy country, full of quiet, laid-back people – rather a quiet and boring nation, in fact. That just goes to show how little they know. If you're thinking of coming to Canada, here are the basics.

THE HISTORY

Europeans arrived in the 1400s but they weren't the first to set sights on this vast land. The earliest known site occupied by people is the Bluefish Caves of the Yukon. In 1000 AD the Vikings from Iceland and Greenland reached the Labrador coast and Newfoundland, but they didn't stay.

It was the North American Indians who greeted the Europeans. As far back as 30,000 BC, the people arrived in North America from Asia by crossing the Bering Strait. These aboriginal people developed distinct languages, customs and religious beliefs. They depended on the land and developed specialised skills to deal with the climate and geography. The Inuit came after the North American Indians (they are not related to them, however) and settled predominantly in the Arctic.

First contacts

French beginnings

In the early 1500s the Spanish, French, British and Italians were all vying to get to North America. The French explorers and missionaries got to Canada first. Jacques Cartier landed at the gulf of the St Lawrence waterway and this led to the founding of New France. It is thought that Canada got its name from Cartier who noticed the Huron and Iroquois inhabitants referring to the land as 'Kanata' which means, 'cluster of dwellings' or 'small community'.

The French had discovered a land rich in natural resources and one of their main activities was fur trading with the native peoples – that is, until the natives realised they were not properly profiting from the trades. The French and natives fought throughout the 1600s because of this and because of the French development of aboriginal land.

Britain steps in

France wasn't all that interested in its new colony even though another of its men, Samuel de Champlain, settled Quebec City and Montreal by 1642. The Hudson's Bay Company was founded in 1670, primarily as a fur trading enterprise (it is Canada's oldest business enterprise, existing today as a major department store chain). The English moved into the Hudson Bay area and by the early 1700s had taken over most of Nova Scotia and Newfoundland. Canada is known as a peacemaking country, but its roots are, like most nations', rooted in war. In 1745 all hell broke loose with the British capture of Fortress Louisbourg from the French. England officially declared war on France in 1756, starting in Europe what is known as the Seven Years' War. Part of that war was played out in Canada.

France v. Britain

The French seemed the stronger nation for four years, but the tide changed in one of Canada's most famous battles. Both the French and English generals died in the battle, but it was the British who defeated the French in 1759 in Quebec on the Plains of Abraham. In 1763 France handed Canada over to Britain in the Treaty of Paris. However, most of Canada's population was French. The conclusion of the Treaty of Paris gave rise to concerns over losing their rights and heritage. In response to these fears, Britain passed the Quebec Act in 1774 which granted religious (Roman Catholic) and linguistic freedom to the French.

But what's history without a little revolution and rebellion? The American Revolution saw Britain's 13 colonies in the south fight for independence from Britain from 1775 to 1783. This led to the migration north to Canada of about 50,000 'Loyalists', so called because of their loyalty to Britain, balancing the number of French and British in Canada. In 1791 Lower Canada (Quebec) and Upper Canada (Ontario) were formed.

Birth of a country

The War of 1812 is often thought to have brought about the beginnings of Canada's national identity. The Americans invaded Canada believing it would be an easy victory. The British, native peoples and French banded together and, although outnumbered, stood their ground. Many battles were won and lost by both sides, but it was their first defence of their country against an invader that saw the people of 'British North America' choose their way of life over that of the republicans to the south. Many heroes and war legends were created. Perhaps one of the least known is that in August 1814, the British captured and burned Washington, including the White House (which in those days wasn't so white and had to be painted white to cover the damage). The war ended in a draw in December 1814 with the Treaty of Ghent.

It wasn't long until the people of Upper and Lower Canada started itching for their own independence. In 1837, rebellions occurred in both colonies, which prompted Britain to join them under a common legislature. Soon afterwards they were granted responsible government and their first taste of political autonomy. More autonomy was on the way with the achievement of Confederation. In 1867 the Dominion of Canada was created under the **British North America Act** (BNA Act) passed by the British government. Sir John A. Macdonald became the first Prime Minister of the Dominion that included Ontario, Quebec, Nova Scotia and New Brunswick. Within the next six years Manitoba, British Columbia and Prince Edward Island were admitted into the Dominion.

The building of the railway

If you come to Canada with children, they will undoubtedly learn in school about the building of the **Canadian Pacific Railway** (CPR). Many scandals erupted during that time, but when it was completed in 1885, the CPR was the longest railway in the world and its construction within five years was considered a great engineering feat. It was built to connect the country from east to west and to encourage settlement. This was met with resistance from the native peoples who were already settled on that land. The aboriginals lost their fight and large numbers of European immigrants came on promises of free land in the west. Between 1881 and 1891, 680,000 people immigrated to Canada and many of them are responsible for the emergence of large-scale grain farming. The South African War, also known as the Boer War, from 1899 to 1902, marked Canada's first official dispatch of troops to an overseas war. In 1904–5 Alberta and Saskatchewan entered Confederation, leaving only Newfoundland on its own.

Modern history

The 1900s saw rapid change due to the industrial revolution: Canada was a significant participant in both World Wars, notably at Vimy Ridge in WW1 and Dieppe and Normandy in WW2, as well as in the air and at sea. English-French tensions continued and the labour movement became organised with the creation of the unions. Canada developed social security programmes such as unemployment insurance, welfare and eventually 'Medicare'. The Canadian Broadcasting Corporation (CBC) was formed and natural resource industries became an integral part of the Canadian economy. Women got the vote, Newfoundland joined the Confederation in 1949 and more than 26,000 Canadians served in the Korean War between 1950 and 1953. In 1965 the Maple Leaf flag was adopted as Canada's national flag.

In 1967 Canada turned 100 years old and celebrated with Expo festivities in Montreal. In the 1970s there was major upheaval in Quebec when the separatist movement took on a violent nature, but in 1980 a referendum showed the majority of Quebecois were against independence. Also in that year, Canada officially adopted *O Canada!* as its national anthem, although the original French version dates from 1880. Speaking of national symbols, the beaver is Canada's national animal.

The last two decades

The eighties were characterised by constitutional issues. Canada's constitution (the **BNA Act**) was an act of the British Parliament and, as an independent country, Canada wanted to 'bring home' the constitution. In 1982, parts of the BNA Act were changed and it became a Canadian act: **The Constitution Act**. Included in it is the **Canadian Charter of Rights and Freedoms**. Quebec is the only province that did not sign the new constitution and two subsequent attempts to bring it in, the Meech Lake Accord and the Charlottetown Accord, failed. In 1995 another Quebec referendum on independence took place and the 'no' side (against independence) won by a very narrow margin.

In the late 1990s, Canada played an important role in trying to bring stability to two areas experiencing serious conflict, namely Kosovo and East Timor.

The terrorist attacks on 11 September 2001 affected the United States directly and most profoundly, but Canada has been impacted as well. Not only on the day of the attacks, when Canada accepted hundreds of air passengers not allowed to land in United States, but also since then in terms of Canada's domestic security policy and foreign policy.

Canada's military mission to Afghanistan began shortly after the attacks. At the time of writing, 71 Canadian soldiers and one diplomat have been killed since the beginning of the mission. It is currently Canada's largest foreign military deployment. There are also missions in the Balkans, the Caribbean, the Middle East and Africa, but Canada declined joining the US in Iraq in 2003.

Other major events in the new millennium include the SARS crisis in Toronto and Vancouver and the hydro-electric blackout in Ontario in the summer of 2003. Also, after much controversy, debate and a Supreme Court decision, parliament made gay marriage legal in 2005. In 2006, Canadians elected the first Conservative government in more than a decade, albeit a minority government, meaning an election is possible at any time.

Inventions and discoveries – in Canada, by Canadians or both

- acrylics
- air-conditioned vehicle
- aircraft de-icer
- antigravity suit
- dental mirror
- electric light bulb (Henry Woodward sold patent to Thomas Edison)
- five-pin bowling
- ginger ale
- lacrosse
- heart pacemaker
- walkie-talkie
- snowshoes
- birch-bark canoe
- winter parka
- mukluks
- kayak
- electron microscope
- canadarm (used on space shuttles)
- pablum (baby cereal)
- instant mashed potatoes
- MacIntosh Apple
- the chocolate bar

- the paint roller
- the telephone (Alexander Graham Bell)
- the wireless photograph transmitter
- the friction match
- the chainsaw
- the snowmobile
- rotating snowplough
- kerosene
- standard time
- the push-up bra
- clothes zipper
- insulin
- battery-less radio
- IMAX technology
- Greenpeace (founded in Vancouver)
- green, plastic garbage bag
- Trivial Pursuit
- ice hockey
- basketball.

Source: Lonely Planet Canada, 1997 and *Made in Canada*

Celebrating identity and diversity

Canada's reputation as a peacekeeping nation has grown through its involvement as a member of the United Nations. It is also a member of the Commonwealth, la Francophonie, the Group of Eight (G8) industrialised nations, the North Atlantic Treaty Organisation (NATO), the North American Aerospace Defence Agreement (NORAD) and the Organisation of American States (OAS).

Canada is a diverse and tolerant nation. Canada as it is known today would not exist if it weren't for immigration, both past and present (see Figure 1). In 2006 more than 250,000 people

Composition of Canada
Top ten ethnic origins

	Number	%
Total population	**29,639,030**	**100***
Canadian	11,682,680	39.4
English	5,978,875	20.2
French	4,668,410	15.8
Scottish	4,157,215	14.0
Irish	3,822,660	12.9
German	2,742,765	9.3
Italian	1,270,369	4.3
Chinese	1,094,700	3.7
Ukranian	1,071,055	3.6
North American Indian	1,000,890	3.4

*Because some respondents reported more than one ethnic origin, the sum is greater than the total population or 100%.

Source: Statistics Canada, 2001 Census

Immigration in 2006
Top ten source countries

	Number	%
Total	135,345	53.8
China	33,080	13.2
India	30,753	12.2
Philippines	17,717	7.0
Pakistan	12,332	4.9
United States	10,943	4.4
Iran	7,073	2.8
United Kingdom	6,542	2.6
Korea	6,178	2.5
Colombia	5,813	2.3
France	4,915	2.0

Source: Citizenship and Immigration Canada

Fig. 1. Canada's immigration statistics.

immigrated to Canada, including both immigrants and refugees. The faces of those who come have changed over the years. During the settlement of the prairies, the immigrants were mainly from Eastern Europe. Leading up to 1961, 25 per cent of immigrants had come from the United Kingdom. Now, a majority of immigrants come from eastern, south-east and southern Asia, although immigration from the UK and the US has begun to increase recently. In the federal government's 2003 Immigration Plan, it is estimated that between 210,000 and 235,000 people will immigrate to Canada. That does not include refugees.

Languages

More than 60 languages are spoken by more than 70 ethnic groups across the country. Multiculturalism became an official government policy in 1971. In 1988, the Government of Canada passed the **Canadian Multiculturalism Act** stating that every citizen, regardless of origin, has an equal chance to participate in all aspects of the country's collective life.

One of Canada's distinguishing qualities is that it is a bilingual country: English and French. When you come to Canada you will discover that even the boxes of cereal tell you the nutritional content in both languages. But, although the country as a whole is officially bilingual, the only province that is officially bilingual is New Brunswick. Quebec sees itself as French-only and the other provinces carry out their business in English. Recently, the city of Moncton, which is in New Brunswick, made itself the first officially bilingual city in Canada. Ottawa, the nation's capital, is not officially bilingual but is considered functionally bilingual.

Another distinguishing mark is that the last thing a Canadian wants to be mistaken for is an American. Canadian culture, attitudes and politics are very different from those of its southern neighbour and Canadians are proud of it.

Religion

Religious freedom is a cornerstone of democracy; many different religions exist and grow within Canada. A large proportion of Canadians are Christian: Catholics and Protestants. Other major religions include Judaism, Islam, Hinduism, Sikhism and Buddhism. However, there's a discrepancy between affiliation and attendance. More than 80 per cent of Canadians say they belong to a religion but only 34 per cent say they attend religious service. And in 2001, about 16 per cent of Canadians said that they had no religious affiliation – up from about 12 per cent in 1981.

IDENTIFYING THE POPULATION

There are a mere 32,612,897 'Canucks'. Ontario and Quebec are the most populous provinces, with Toronto and Montreal the largest cities. Montreal followed Toronto's lead recently, becoming what is known as an amalgamated city. Amalgamation sees many of the city's suburbs join onto the city proper to become one giant mega-city. Ottawa and the Ontario cities have also been forced to amalgamate. Amalgamation has been controversial with residents quite opposed, but with the provincial governments going ahead with it anyway, claiming it will reduce costs (it hasn't). But, amalgamation has meant the new Toronto can now claim to be one of the largest cities in North America, with a population of 5.1 million.

Province/Territory	Population	Capital City
Newfoundland and Labrador	506,469	St. John's
Prince Edward Island	135,851	Charlottetown
Nova Scotia	913,462	Halifax
New Brunswick	729,997	Fredericton
Quebec	7,546,131	Quebec City
Ontario	12,160,282	Toronto
Manitoba	1,148,401	Winnipeg
Saskatchewan	968,933	Regina
Alberta	3,290,350	Edmonton
British Columbia	4,113,487	Victoria
Yukon	30,372	Whitehorse
Northwest Territories	41,464	Yellowknife
Nunavut	29,474	Iqaluit

Source: Statistics Canada, 2006 estimate

UNDERSTANDING THE GOVERNMENT

Canada is a constitutional monarchy. Queen Elizabeth II is
Canada's official head of state. The **Governor General** is her
representative in Canada, although in many ways the Governor
General's role is largely symbolic. Officially, the Governor General
is appointed by the Queen on the advice of the Prime Minister. In
Canada, powers and responsibilities are divided between the
federal government and the provincial and territorial governments.
If a bill is defeated in either a provincial legislature or in the
House of Commons, the government in power is usually forced to
call an election, as the defeat represents non-confidence.

Three tiers of government

Federal government

The **federal government** is based in Ottawa, chosen to be the capital of Canada as a compromise between Toronto and Montreal and because Kingston was too close to the US (and the war of 1812 was still pretty fresh in the Queen's memory). Parliament has an elected **House of Commons** and an appointed **Senate**. The House of Commons is the national legislature that approves all legislation. The Senate is the Upper House that gives a 'sober second thought' to legislation. The final stamp of approval on a bill comes from 'royal assent' given by the Governor General, although a Governor General has never refused a bill, which is why the role is seen as symbolic.

There are several political parties; the one that wins the most seats (out of 308) in an election forms the federal government. The leader of that party becomes the Prime Minister who chooses the Cabinet from the Members of Parliament (MPs) in that party. Each Cabinet Minister has a particular portfolio to oversee. The party that gets the second most seats forms the Official Opposition and its leader becomes the Leader of the Opposition. Canadian citizens can vote at 18. The governing party's term is a maximum of five years. But the Prime Minister can, and often does, call an election before that time.

However, parliament has passed legislation that will see a fixed election date every four years, unless there is a minority government (when the opposition parties still have the power to bring down the government). At the time of writing, that new bill was simply awaiting royal assent to come into force. That would mean an upcoming election date of October 19, 2009, unless the current minority government falls before then.

Several provinces and one territory have changed to having fixed election dates including British Columbia, Ontario, PEI, Newfoundland and Labrador and the Northwest Territories. Others are considering it as well.

The federal government is responsible for such matters as defence, criminal law, banking and foreign relations.

Provincial/territorial government

The provinces each have their own governments with certain responsibilities. The provincial legislatures do not have a Senate. For legislation to become law, the provincial assembly and the **Lieutenant Governor** (the Queen's provincial representative) must approve it, just as the Governor General does with federal legislation. Parliament delegates powers to the territories; the territories are not sovereign units but they have elected assemblies run very much like those of the provinces.

The provinces are responsible for health, education, property and civil justice. They pay for those responsibilities through provincial taxes (which the provincial government has the right to raise or lower) and transfer payments from the federal government. Some provinces, unfortunately known as the 'have not' provinces, receive equalisation payments from the federal government (although that money is generated from the 'have' provinces, which are Ontario and Alberta).

Local government
Municipal governments run things most immediate in people's lives: schools, local transport, police, etc. They are elected regularly but do not have constitutional powers. The higher governments, usually the provincial level, delegate to them their responsibilities. This set-up has led to many conflicts between city governments and the provincial and federal governments. The provinces have downloaded responsibilities like social housing onto the cities. But city governments do not have the same revenue-generating capabilities as the provinces and can raise only property taxes and user fees. At the same time, more and more people are moving into the cities and city governments are finding it hard to cope. There has been much talk about creating a 'new deal for cities' but nothing has happened yet.

THE LEGAL AND JUDICIAL SYSTEMS

Canada's legal system is based both on English common law and the French civil code. In nine out of ten provinces the laws are determined by legal precedents, not by written statutes. In Quebec, however, civil law applies which is based on a written code that contains general principles and rules.

Canada has several levels of courts both at the provincial and federal levels. Each province has its own court of appeal and there is also a court of appeal for the federal level. The judiciary is independent; judges are appointed by the provincial and federal governments but are not beholden to government agendas in any way. **The Supreme Court of Canada** is the highest court in the country. It has the final decision on any matter pertaining to law in Canada, including interpreting constitutional questions. There are nine Supreme Court justices, three of whom must be from the province of Quebec.

The RCMP, or the **Royal Canadian Mounted Police**, is Canada's national police force. The RCMP is headed by a commissioner, but the Solicitor General (a cabinet minister in the federal government) oversees the organisation. One hundred years ago, it started as a small rural force. Now it comprises 17,000 peace officers and about 6,000 civilian employees. Widely recognised by the world as red-coated, broad-hatted officers on horseback, Mounties are responsible for the following:

- Acting as the municipal force in about 200 cities and towns.

- Providing provincial police services in all provinces and territories other than Ontario and Quebec, which have their own provincial forces.

- Enforcing 140 laws and statutes dealing with serious crimes.

- Representing Canada as a member of the International Criminal Police Organisation (INTERPOL).

- Enforcing national security (although in 1984 the Canadian Security Intelligence Service, CSIS, took over the RCMP's intelligence-gathering responsibilities).

Many municipalities, especially the large urban centres, have their own police forces. Overall in 2006, there was one police officer for every 507 Canadians. The number of police officers in Canada has been on a slight rise over the last few years, mostly due to an increase in the number of RCMP officers. But it is still lower than the United States and England. Both those countries have an officer for approximately every 240 people.

LOOKING AT GEOGRAPHY AND CLIMATE

Okay, so you know Canada is big, but many people really can't grasp just how large it is until they visit. Canada has a landmass of 9,970,610 km^2 making it the second-largest country in the world after Russia. Yet because it has a population of only about 32 million, it has one of the smallest population densities in the world: three persons per square kilometre.

Until 1 April 1999, Canada was made up of ten **provinces** and two **territories**, but on that day the map was changed when the Northwest Territories was divided in two to create a third territory: Nunavut. Eighty-five per cent of Nunavut's population is Inuit. Nunavut means 'our land' in Inuktitut, the Inuit language. This had been a long-time dream for the Inuit of the NWT. The new Nunavut government oversees land of about two million square kilometres.

The border between Canada and the United States is 8,892 km and it has coastlines on the Atlantic, Pacific and Arctic Oceans. That means it has the longest coastline of any country. The Arctic islands come within 800 km of the North Pole.

The landscapes and climates in Canada are remarkably varied. No, it isn't all snow and ice, but because a great deal of Canada is in a harsh northern climate, ninety per cent of the population live within a few hundred kilometres of the US border.

Canada has one-seventh of the world's fresh water made up from the Great Lakes and the infinite number of large and small rivers and lakes throughout the country. It has almost everything: flat plains, high mountain peaks, green valleys, beaches, cliffs, etc.

Canadian regions

Canada has seven distinct geographic regions:

◆ The **Pacific Coast** has a temperate climate. There you find rain forests and the oldest trees in Canada: 1,300-year-old western red cedars and 90m high Douglas firs.

◆ The **Cordillera** stretches from British Columbia to just east of the Alberta border. The Rocky Mountains, the Coast Mountains and the Elias Mountains are the main attractions. Canada's highest point, mount Logan (6,050m) is in part of the Elias range in the Yukon.

◆ The **Prairies** are known for their endless wheat fields and for having very few trees. Some of the largest concentrations of dinosaur fossils in the world have been found in this dry region that is also famous for its petroleum production.

◆ The **Canadian Shield** wraps around the Hudson Bay. It is a rocky region that reaches as far east as Labrador, south to Lake Ontario and northwest to the Arctic Ocean. Its granite rock is 3.5 billion years old; this region has been the stage for most of Canada's mining. But it is also home to boreal forest of spruce, fir, tamarack and pine.

◆ The **Great Lakes** – St Lawrence Lowlands contain Canada's two largest cities, Montreal and Toronto. It is prime growing land for fruits and vegetables and even the odd vineyard. This is also one of the most photographed regions in the autumn time when all the leaves change colour.

◆ The **Atlantic Provinces-Appalachian** region contains the four smallest Canadian provinces (the Maritime Provinces). It is also prime agricultural land and gets quite a bit of precipitation.

♦ The **Arctic** is north of the tree line. It has nearly continuous daylight during its short summer as well as some fairly warm temperatures that help the flowers bloom on the tundra. But the winters are long, cold and at their depth, very dark indeed.

Canadian climate

Canada is a country of extremes. Some cities can see lows of −30° in the winter and yet highs of +30° in the summertime. The West Coast can be mild but gets a lot of rain. The prairies are dry in the summer but cold and snowy in the winter. Central Canada sees a bit of variety. Toronto's winters are not nearly as harsh as those of Ottawa, Montreal or Quebec City – you could see temperatures as low as −50° in Quebec City – but both Toronto and Montreal have quite hot and humid summers. The east usually isn't very hot in the summer but can be snowy and cold in the winter.

You should know that technically spring is March, April and May, summer is June to August, autumn/fall is September to November and winter is December to February. However, practically speaking it doesn't always work out that way. And more and more, the norms are not really the norms. As in much of the world, Canada is seeing its weather go topsy-turvy. In the summer of 2002, parts of the prairies suffered extreme drought, while other parts were flooded. Parts of Alberta had snowfall right into June and southwestern Ontario had its hottest summer on record. Whether you blame it on global warming or not, the weather isn't always predictable. Still, the chart in Figure 2 will help make sense of it all. Remember, however, that the following are averages and on any given day, temperatures can be much lower or much higher (for example: the coldest day on record in Iqaluit is −46°, the warmest 24.4°).

**Average coldest and warmest temperatures
(in degrees Celsius) in capital and major cities**

City	Average lowest temp/month	Average highest temp/month
St John's	-8.7/February	20.2/July
Charlottetown	-12.2/January	23.1/July
Halifax	-10.6/February	23.4/July
Fredericton	-15.4/January	25.6/July
Quebec City	-17.3/January	24.9/July
Montreal	-14.9/January	26.2/July
Ottawa	-15.5/January	26.4/July
Toronto	-7.9/January	26.5/July
Winnipeg	-23.6/January	26.1/July
Regina	-22.1/January	26.3/July
Edmonton	-17 /January	23.0/July
Calgary	-15.7/January	23.2/July
Vancouver	0.1/January	21.7/August
Victoria	0.3/January	21.8/July
Whitehorse	-23.2/January	20.3/July
Yellowknife	-32.2/January	20.8/July
Iqaluit	-31.0/February	11.6/July

Fig. 2. Canada's climate.

It might help to compare the temperatures in Figure 2 with those in other capitals. London, England, for example, has an average low of 5° in January and February and an average high of 23° in July. Paris, France sees its low in January at 4° and its high at 24° in July.

When you hear of excessively cold temperatures in Canadian cities, it's usually due to something called the **wind-chill factor**. The wind-chill makes the actual temperature feel much colder. You'll hear the weather people saying that it's –10° but feels like

−25° with the wind-chill. At times like those, you'll also hear warnings about how long skin can go unprotected before frostbite kicks in. This is something to take very seriously. They don't make featherdown and waterproof jackets for nothing.

On the hottest days the weather forecasters will tell you that 'with the **humidex** it's 30'. This reading takes into account the humidity level, which in cities like Toronto and Montreal can make a big difference. That's when you're grateful for air conditioning.

In both summer and winter on very sunny days, forecasters will warn you of the UV index. High levels from seven upwards means skin will sunburn quickly.

THE ECONOMY

Over the last few years, Canada's economy has often outperformed those of the other G8 countries, which include France, Germany, Japan, Italy, USA, Russia and the UK. In fact, Canada has recovered from the latest global downturn at a much faster pace than even the US.

Annual growth in 2006 was at 2.7 per cent. Estimates put growth for 2007 at 2.3 per cent and forecasts for 2008 put growth at 2.8 per cent. Inflation has hovered around the one to two per cent range for years now, partly because it has been a primary goal of the Bank of Canada to keep it low. For years, interest rates were at record low levels as the Bank had consistently lowered them to ward off recession. But with a booming economy, the Bank has been raising the rate slowly to keep inflation low. Rates are still low, relatively speaking. At the time of writing the rate was set at 4.5 per cent (although banks lend money at a higher rate than the

Bank of Canada's rate). Unemployment has been declining since 1994, when it was 10.4 per cent, to a present day 30-year low of 6.1 per cent.

Canada's biggest trading partner is the United States which accounts for more than 85 per cent of exports. In the past years, however, the two countries have feuded over a number of trade issues and agreements, most notably over softwood lumber and US farming subsidies. Natural resources are a large part of Canada's exports to the US, but Canada is also a leader in aerospace engineering.

Assessing living expenses

The cost of living in Canada is not unreasonably high but, because of higher taxes, which pay for social services, consumer goods are not as cheap as in the US or Mexico, though they are quite a bit cheaper than in the UK or France. Regular unleaded gasoline prices in the middle of 2007 were $1.02 per litre. In the UK the average at time of writing was $2.09 per litre (prices are shown in Canadian dollars). In the US it was $3.25 a litre (although in the US gas is bought by the gallon). In Canada, gas prices tend to fluctuate, and also vary across the country. For example, gas is more expensive further north and in Quebec. For housing, automobile and education costs, see the appropriate chapters.

The Canadian dollar continues to trade poorly against the British pound, but has recently soared against the US dollar. It trades poorly against the Euro, but well against the Australian dollar. Currently the exchange rate is approximately $2.16 = £1 and $1.06 = $1 US.

In 2005, family expenditure for a household (two or more people) averaged $66,857, with 20 per cent on personal income taxes, 19 per cent on shelter and 11 per cent on food, 14 per cent on transportation and 36 per cent on other things. Those other things include recreation, personal insurance and pension contributions, household operations, clothing, gifts, entertainment and contributions to charity. The lowest income households spent a much greater proportion of income on shelter and a much smaller proportion on personal income taxes.

Nearly 60 per cent of Canadians own their own homes. Ninety-nine per cent of homes have telephone service. The long-distance market is very competitive, with overseas rates as low as 5¢ per minute to the UK, 5¢ to the US and within Canada and 7¢ to Hong Kong. In fact, most markets in Canada are very competitive which keeps prices low.

Banking

The federal government regulates all banks and most trust companies. Banks are also members of the Canadian Deposit Insurance Corporation (CDIC), so your deposits are insured up to $60,000. To open an account you will need proper identification, such as one or more of the following: a bank card from a reputable financial institution, a credit card, passport and a Canadian driver's licence.

Not having a job or a minimum deposit should not prevent you from opening an account, although the bank might do a credit check to determine such things as your daily withdrawal limit with a bank card or whether to hold deposited cheques until they clear.

When opening an account, you will have to sign an account agreement that outlines the rules of the accounts, what kind of account you are opening (chequeing, savings etc.), account number, interest to be paid on the account, service charges etc.

If a problem arises with your bank that cannot be resolved directly with them (a serious attempt must be made), you can contact the Canadian Banking Ombudsman (see Useful Addresses).

The national debt

One of Canada's problems, however, continues to be its national debt. Currently it stands at $481.5 billion. However, that's down from previous years due to the fact the federal government has reported budget surpluses in the billions for seven years in a row. The government uses a large part of those surpluses to pay off the debt and it is hoped that with the elimination of yearly deficits, which had been the standard since the 1970s, Canada can chip away at the debt, eventually lower taxes and put more money into social services instead of interest payments.

ATTITUDES

It is difficult to generalise about a nation's attitudes. Generally, however, Canadians are concerned about the environment, enjoy the outdoors and take human rights very seriously. They understand the importance of democracy and the value of their right to vote. However, voter apathy is on the rise. In the 2006 federal election only 64.7 per cent of Canadians cast their ballots, one of the lowest turnouts in recent Canadian history. In the 1980s, voter turnout averaged 73 per cent.

Canadians work hard, but consider their jobs just one part of life. Family time, sports, recreation and the arts are important too. Which is why there is much grumbling about lack of vacation time in Canada compared to other countries, especially Europe. On average, a Canadian will get two weeks off a year, in addition to special holiday days, like Christmas and Canada Day.

Canadians believe in equality, as outlined in the **Charter of Rights and Freedoms**. Women have made great gains in equality in the work place – but inequalities still exist. Similarly, people of different racial groups and physical capabilities are protected from discrimination under law, but that is not to say that discrimination doesn't exist. All in all, Canada is a pleasant country that is accepting and easy-going. It is not difficult to adapt to life here; most people enjoy visiting, living and working in Canada.

3

Immigration to Canada

UNDERSTANDING POLICY AND POLITICS

The political, economic, and legal climates in Canada are
constantly shifting when it comes to immigration, both temporary
and permanent. As in many parts of the world, there is a
movement towards restricting access to Canada for immigrants,
but there are also countervailing economic and social realities.
Indeed, Canadian immigration law was altered on 28 June 2002
generally making the rules more restrictive. By contrast, certain
programmes regarding temporary entry have been made less
restrictive – for instance for computer professionals – recognising
the realities of the economic demand in this sector. As such,
though we hope to provide accurate, up-to-date information about
Canadian immigration law and policy, you must investigate
matters pertaining to your own case with the appropriate
government office or professional at the time that you seek
immigration, permanent or temporary. Further, Canadian
immigration law covers volumes and volumes, which obviously
cannot be condensed into just one chapter, so discussion, though
as thorough as possible, is obviously limited.

There are a few important principles of which you should be
aware, for an understanding of our immigration policies and
philosophies. An understanding of these will often lead to a better
understanding of the underlying law and regulations, and
therefore the guidelines which will affect you.

Guiding principles

There are a number of principles set out in Canada's Immigration Act. Canada's immigration laws are designed to promote, for example:

+ cultural and social enrichment;
+ trade and commerce through temporary entry of visitors;
+ Canada's international humanitarian obligations;
+ a strong and viable economy;
+ maintenance of Canadian society's health, safety and security.

These basic principles are then moulded to fit specific issues. With regard to entry for **temporary workers**, the philosophy is 'net benefit to Canada'; that is to say, does an applicant provide Canada with some benefit to justify the hiring of a foreign worker? Contrast this with the philosophy pursuant to the previous law which was 'Canadians first'. As will be discussed below, this leads to various procedures required to satisfy immigration officials before a foreign worker will be entitled to enter and work in Canada, and also an elaborate system of exceptions which must be considered.

With regard to **permanent residence**, the guiding principles go on to shape the criteria employed for selection of immigrants. Indeed, recognising demographics, commerce, and other issues, Canada promotes immigration, though in recent times there sometimes appears to be a harsher attitude among those making the selection decisions. Canada's Federal Court is full of cases of rejected immigration applicants and there appears to be no let-up in sight.

With this in mind, let us explore some of the issues in Canadian immigration.

ILLEGAL IMMIGRATION

Before looking at the general issues involved in getting into, or staying in, Canada, it is important to realise that violation of Canadian immigration law could have severe consequences. We will discuss below the various programmes and policies affecting immigration to Canada which will allow people to come to, and remain in, Canada. Certainly, however, in the last few years, there has been a rise in illegal immigration to Canada, and the authorities are taking an increasingly harsh position against people caught in this position. If you attempt to enter Canada without the appropriate legal authorisation and documentation, you will meet a stern turn-around from Canadian immigration authorities, whether before you board the plane or after you land, wherever the problem is detected. Canadian immigration authorities are now conducting checks of persons at airports abroad before people can even board the plane.

Similarly, someone already in Canada who breaches Canadian immigration or criminal law will face possible deportation. Meeting the requirements of Canadian immigration is no laughing matter, and the consequences of failing to obey the rules could lead to deportation and the inability to return to Canada ever again.

KNOWING THE GENERAL REQUIREMENTS

If you are seeking to enter Canada, you should ensure that all proper requirements are met. These may include:

♦ Obtaining a visa before arriving, for certain nationalities. The list changes from time to time – see Figure 3 for the current list.

A Canadian Visa Post should be consulted if there is any question.

♦ Ensuring that there is no criminal bar to entry – a criminal record could lead to denial of entry to Canada for permanent or temporary purposes.

♦ Ensuring that there is no medical inadmissibility issue – the existence of an ailment which could jeopardise Canadian health and safety, or be a burden on our health system, could lead to inadmissibility.

♦ Further, specific requirements may be needed in particular instances, such as a work permit for those seeking to work in Canada.

We give you here the basic idea about the legal issues involved in the process. Once you feel that you may qualify under one of the areas discussed, you will have to deal with the procedures involved. You will need to:

♦ obtain the appropriate forms

♦ look at the practical issues involved in submitting an application

♦ and ascertain the proper documentation required from a Canadian Visa Post or legal adviser.

Canada divides the type of people entering the country into two basic groups – **temporary** and **permanent** – both of which are discussed on page 41.

Afghanistan	Grenada	Nicaragua
Albania	Guatemala	Niger
Algeria	Guinea	Nigeria
Angola	Guinea-Bissau	Oman
Argentina	Guyana	Pakistan
Armenia	Haiti	Palau
Azerbaijan	Honduras	Palestinian Authority
Bahrain	Hungary	Panama
Bangladesh	India	Paraguay
Belarus	Indonesia	Peru
Belize	Iran	Philippines
Benin	Iraq	Poland
Bhutan	Israel (only Israeli	Qatar
Bolivia	citizens holding	Romania
Bosnia-Herzegovina	valid Israeli 'Travel	Russia
Brazil	Document in lieu of	Rwanda
Bulgaria	National Passport')	Sao Tomé e Principe
Burkina-Faso	Ivory Coast	Saudi Arabia
Burundi	Jamaica	Senegal
Cambodia	Jordan	Serbia
Cameroon	Kazakhstan	Seychelles, The
Cape Verde	Kenya	Sierra Leone
Central African	Kirabati	Slovak Republic
Republic	Korea, North	Somalia
Chad	Kuwait	South Africa
Chile	Kyrgyzstan	Sri Lanka
China	Laos	Sudan
Colombia	Latvia	Surinam
Comoros	Lebanon	Syria
Congo, Democratic	Lesotho	Taiwan
Republic	Liberia	Tajikistan
Congo, People's	Libya	Tanzania
Republic	Lithuania	Thailand
Costa Rica	Macao S.A.R.	Togo
Croatia	Macedonia	Tonga
Cuba	Madagascar	Trinidad and Tobago
Czech Republic	Malawi	Tunisia
Djibouti	Malaysia	Turkey
Dominica	Maldives	Turkmenistan
Dominican Republic	Mali	Tuvalu
East Timor	Marshall Islands	Uganda
Ecuador	Mauritania	Ukraine
Egypt	Mauritius	United Arab Emirates
El Salvador	Micronesia	Uruguay
Equatorial Guinea	Moldova	Uzbekistan
Eritrea	Mongolia	Vanuatu
Ethiopia	Montenegro	Venezuela
Fiji	Morocco	Vietnam
Gabon	Mozambique	Yemen
Gambia	Myanmar (Burma)	Yugoslavia
Georgia	Naura	Zambia
Ghana	Nepal	Zimbabwe

Fig. 3. Countries whose citizens need visas.

TEMPORARY VISA ISSUES

Temporary entry can be broken down further into three branches:

- **temporary residents (formerly 'visitors')**
- **students**
- **foreign workers.**

There are exceptional circumstances which can give rise to entry on other grounds (through, for instance, a **Temporary Resident Permit** where someone may not otherwise be admissible), but these are the basic categories. It should be noted that even for those people for whom the student or worker categories seem applicable, the issues relating to temporary residents discussed below relate as well and should be considered.

Temporary residents/'visitors'

Visitors are temporary residents who come to Canada neither to study nor work. Visiting can of course have various purposes, from the simplest form of someone who is just a tourist, to those coming for a business visit. Anyone who is not a student or worker will be put into this broad category.

Technically, anyone seeking to come to Canada as a visitor must obtain a **temporary resident visa** at a Canadian Visa Post (Embassy, Consulate or High Commission dealing with immigration matters) before entering Canada. Nationals of certain countries, including the United Kingdom, have been exempted from this requirement (see Figure 3 for list of countries requiring visas). However, this does not mean that British citizens, as just one example of a visa-exempt country, are immune from the enforcement of Canadian immigration law. Indeed, anyone appearing at a Canadian port of entry (anywhere where one enters Canada, either at an airport, sea port, or land crossing) must justify his or her entitlement to enter Canada, and may be questioned as to the reason for seeking entry.

Denying entry

Canadian immigration officials have the right to deny entry whenever they feel that it would be in violation of Canadian immigration law, for instance, in a case where there is concern that the person may be inadmissible due to a criminal problem, or if there is concern that the person would not leave at the end of the visitation period (often granted for six months initially). Without reviewing all grounds for inadmissibility (which are numerous), persons seeking to enter Canada should be aware that certain issues are foremost in the minds of Canadian immigration officers when determining whether to allow entry of a foreign national. A criminal history, as noted above, is an important reason for entry being denied, and virtually any prior criminal history will be caught in the dragnet of Canadian legislation. Medical grounds can also lead to refusal of admission to Canada, based on a threat to the Canadian public or a possible burden on the Canadian health system.

Obtaining a visa does not stop an immigration officer from denying entry. It does, however, allow the person concerned to 'pre-screen' any contentious issues, and give some later flexibility.

Students

In addition to the issues discussed above, those wishing to study in Canada must meet some further requirements, and must generally obtain the visa for studying before arriving in Canada. First, a student must have an acceptance to a Canadian educational institution. Certain institutions will not qualify, and it will be necessary to check with a Canadian Visa Post or immigration professional before making application.

As a student, you will also have to demonstrate your ability to support yourself while in Canada – perhaps with a sum of some $10,000 to $15,000 or more – and the intention to return when studies are concluded. It is again important to note that a student visa is temporary and applicants must convince an officer that it is not their intention to remain in Canada permanently. That being said, it is possible to extend student visas after arriving in Canada, as the educational programme proceeds from year to year or other time frame, or if there is a change of institution. Eventually, however, the visa will end.

Students in some cases will also be entitled to a non-renewable one-year or two-year work permit at the conclusion of their programme to work in their field of study.

See also the discussion in Chapter 8 about some of the exchange programmes and other student-specific programmes for coming to Canada.

Foreign workers
This is perhaps the most asked about, and misunderstood, aspect of Canadian immigration. People often say, if they can't get permanent residence, they will just come to work temporarily. Unfortunately, it's not that easy. A **temporary work permit** is not a substitute for permanent residence, or a lesser form of

permanent residence. It is sometimes more difficult to get a temporary work permit than permanent residence. See also Chapter 7 for information about working in Canada.

The usual process
Subject to exemptions discussed later (which should be tried first when possible), the general procedure to obtain a work permit is as follows.

Canada's policy, as indicated, is 'net benefit to Canada'. A foreigner can work in Canada only when this is justified, and may include issues as to whether there is no Canadian to fill a position. Therefore the process begins with the employer.

According to the legislation which took effect 28 June 2002, an employer must establish a number of factors to an officer of Service Canada (formerly Human Resources and Social Development Canada) before a **'positive labour market opinion'** (also referred to as a Confirmation) can be provided, which is the precursor to a work permit application. The Service Canada officer will consider factors including:

◆ whether the work is likely to result in direct job creation or job retention for Canadians (Canadians includes citizens and permanent residents);

◆ whether the work is likely to result in the creation or transfer of skills and knowledge for the benefit of Canadians;

◆ whether the work is likely to fill a labour shortage;

◆ whether the wages and working conditions offered are sufficient; to attract and retain Canadians;

♦ whether the employer has made or has agreed to make reasonable efforts to hire or train Canadians;

♦ whether the employment of the foreign national is likely to adversely affect settlement of a labour dispute.

Once Service Canada provides a positive Labour Market Opinion, a foreign worker may then proceed to apply for a work permit at the appropriate Canadian Visa Post (or in some cases, port of entry). The worker will need to substantiate that his or her credentials meet the requirements of the job in question. Obviously, as well, a temporary work permit is indeed temporary, generally issued for an initial period of one year, and renewable thereafter – if the reason for the renewal can be substantiated.

Based on the structure of the programme, the reality is that the less sophisticated a job or an applicant's credentials, the less likely that Confirmation and/or work permit will be granted, since it is less likely that there are no Canadians to fill the position.

Typically, the occupations permitted are considered NOC 0, A, or B. Though somewhat beyond the scope of this book, NOC is the National Occupational Classification. All occupations are placed on a grid and '0' level are management positions; A and B are high level – usually requiring a university degree – occupations (more information about NOC and the categorisation of occupations can be found at http://www23.hrdc-drhc.gc.ca/2001/e/generic/matrix.pdf). Service Canada, however, does now offer a 'low skilled worker pilot project' (NOC C and D) which will allow employers to seek a Confirmation for up to two years in regard to applicants for lower level occupations. There are a number of conditions to be met in this regard, and perhaps most notably, a sustained attempt to look for persons for the position.

Service Canada now also recognises that some occupations in some geographical locations are in demand. In Alberta, British Columbia and Ontario, there are now 'occupations under pressure' lists, which will allow for slightly relaxed criteria to search for foreign workers in those fields.

Information on Service Canada programmes generally can be found at http://www.hrsdc.gc.ca/en/workplaceskills/ foreign_workers/index.shtml with further branches for specific programmes, such as the occupations under pressure.

The exemptions
As noted earlier, sometimes there are exceptions to the rules of when a Labour Market Opinion, or even a work permit itself, will be required.

With regard to categories of persons not requiring work permits, these are listed in the regulations to the Canadian Immigration and Refugee Protection Act. Some examples are: foreign journalists, certain clergy, certain athletes participating in events in Canada, diplomats, certain performing artists, foreign crew members and certain members of foreign armed forces. Business visitors may also enter for a limited time, as may employees of a corporation with a foreign component who are in Canada to consult with other members of the organisation.

◆ Proper counselling as to whether your occupation is available for work permit exemption should be sought when applicable, due to changing procedures, requirements and definitions.

With regard to those exempt from the need for a Labour Market Opinion, sometimes some creativity will be required. There are provisions, for instance, in Canadian law to argue that someone shouldn't need to go through the Service Canada process where they are creating or maintaining jobs in Canada ('significant benefit') – so where the XYZ company in Toronto needs a specialist to repair its new high-tech machine for employees to get back to work, the Visa Post can be approached directly and the argument made. Similarly, someone with specialised knowledge or management capacity can obtain a working permit without a Labour Market Opinion as an intra-company transferee. At this time there are also programmes which specifically eliminate the need for individual Labour Market Opinions in certain occupations – most notably computer professionals. In this case, where a person meets certain job descriptions set out by the Canadian government in the computer field, a simple job offer will do the trick to allow for a work permit, as Service Canada has issued a 'Blanket Confirmation' for these people. Again, care should be taken in determining if the Blanket Confirmation applies, since the job definitions applicable are limited, as is the time frame for the existence of the programme.

There are numerous other times where the need for a Labour Market Opinion can be avoided, and these should obviously be explored wherever possible. Other examples may include people carrying out certain research, and intra-company transferees.

International agreements
Certain international treaties and instruments now also lead to more lenient processing of temporary work permits in some cases.

For instance, Canada is now a party to the following international agreements:

♦ GATS – the General Agreement on Trade in Services (a cousin to the more famous GATT), to which both Canada and the UK are signatories.

♦ NAFTA – the North American Free Trade Agreement, to which Canada, the United States and Mexico are signatories.

♦ CCFTA – the Canada-Chile Free Trade Agreement, to which Canada and Chile are signatories.

Though each of these is different, there are some common elements to the immigration provisions in the documents. Each agreement provides for nationals of signatory states to enter the territory of the other for the purpose of working, and in particular in certain categories including intra-corporate transferees, business visitors and professionals.

General agreement allowances
As noted, certain types of workers generally fall under these agreements and there are some similar characteristics. Appropriate legal advice should be sought about the specific requirements of any one agreement and the application of the agreement to your situation.

♦ An **intra-corporate transferee** is someone who has an executive or managerial level position in an organisation, or who has specialised knowledge in the organisation and is being transferred to a related company in Canada. Note that the rules regarding required length of previous service in the company, job specifications, relationship of foreign and Canadian companies and other matters vary from situation to situation, and specific advice must be sought when use of one of these agreements is being considered.

◆ A **business visitor** is someone coming to Canada to conduct business affairs on behalf of a foreign entity in a signatory state, where that person will not directly enter the work force. Indeed, no work permit may actually be required – just a record of the reason for entry. Generally, the person may be marketing services or establishing a commercial entity.

◆ A **professional** is someone coming to Canada to work in his profession; each agreement has a list of accredited professions from the other signatory countries who may work in Canada, if invited by a Canadian company to do so, but who must meet the eligibility to work in that profession in Canada (such as licensing issues). Examples of some professions, under NAFTA, for instance, are: accountant, graphic designer, urban planner, librarian, lawyer, veterinarian, geologist, physicist. Reference must be made to the specific agreement for your particular case.

Special programmes

Canada also implements, from time to time, certain special programmes to allow foreign workers to come to Canada. For instance, there is a programme which allows farm workers from Mexico and certain Caribbean countries to enter Canada during agricultural harvest periods. There are exchange programmes in some high-tech fields. There is also at this time the IT Workers Programme as previously noted, which allows easier entry for computer programmers in certain specific programming fields to enter with a Blanket Labour Market Opinion (see 'the usual process' above).

Contact your nearest Canadian Visa Post or a legal representative to see if there is a specific programme in place for your field at this time.

Extension of status
Once in Canada, it is your obligation to extend your visa prior to its expiry – usually about one month pre-expiry. At that time, it is necessary to justify the need for your extension of the visitor, study or work permit. Failure to extend the visa may result in removal proceedings, as legal status has expired. Applications for extension are made through the Canada Immigration Centre in Vegreville, Alberta, and applications can be obtained by calling a local Canada immigration telephone number, found in the blue pages of most Canadian telephone books, or through www.cic.gc.ca the Canadian Government Immigration website.

OBTAINING PERMANENT RESIDENCE

For many hundreds of thousands, if not millions of people around the world, Canadian **permanent residence status** is a dream. Proper pre-assessment and guidance can make that dream become a reality. This aspect of Canadian immigration law is susceptible to change, and proposals are currently in place to change the criteria affecting selection. The information provided here is up to date at the time of writing.

Skilled worker immigration
The most common method of obtaining Canadian permanent residence is through what is often referred to as the 'skilled worker system'. Under law enacted 28 June 2002, the following factors are considered in this category:

- **Age**: maximum points are 10 if aged 21–49, with 2 points deducted for each year above or below.

- **Education**: maximum points are 25. 5 points for secondary education which could lead to higher education, 15 points for most trade school or community college credentials, 20 points for a university degree, and 25 points for a Master's Degree or higher (there are further breakdowns, but these are the most common categories).

- **Arranged employment**: 10 points if Service Canada approves a job offer, or in some cases, if you are currently working in Canada. (This is different from a labour market opinion discussed above.)

- **First official language**: generally this will be English for readers of this book. 16 points maximum 'with high proficiency' in reading, writing, listening and speaking.

- **Second official language**: generally this will be French, for which a maximum of 8 points is available. (Note: depending on levels of fluency, English and French can be reversed.)

- **Experience**: maximum 21 for 4 years or more in a field listing in categories Ø, A or B of the National Occupation Classification (NOC). (For more information, see page 45.) Though somewhat beyond the scope of this book, NOC is the National Occupational Classification; all occupations are placed on a grid and '0' level are management positions; A and B are high level – usually university degree requiring – occupations (more information about NOC and the categorisation of occupations can be found at http://www23.hrdc-drhc.gc.ca/2001/e/generic/matrix.pdf).

◆ **Adaptability**: this factor is composed of five sub-elements (note that the maximum available is 10 points):
5 points are available for previous study in Canada
5 points are available for previous work in Canada
5 points are available for having a close relative in Canada
up to 5 points (of the spouse 5 points) are available for the educational credential of the spouse of the principal applicant

◆ 5 (additional) points for having arranged employment.

A total of 67 points must be achieved, subject to the further discretion of the immigration officer to grant visas to those with less than 67 points, or refuse visas to those with more than 67 points.

Furthermore, you must provide evidence of 'settlement funds' – sufficient funds to show that you and any dependants can take care of yourselves for the first few months after arrival in Canada. It is expected that, on average, a family will take six months to settle in, and in particular to find employment and begin active life in Canada.

A quick summary chart to work out your own score is given in Figure 4. Note that this is a simple, general form only, as is the information above. You must contact a Canadian Visa Post or appropriate legal adviser for up-to-date information about the issues in an application for permanent residence.

Note that Canada Immigration has implemented at all visa posts (except Buffalo) a 'simplified application process' whereby applicants submit only a skeleton application until the visa post is ready to process – which, depending on the post, can be a few

Factor	Maximum Score	Your Score
Age:	10	
Education:	25	
Arranged employment:	10	
Experience:	21	
First official language:	16	
Second official language:	8	
Adaptability		
Previous study in Canada:	5	
Previous work in Canada:	5	
Relative in Canada:	5	
Spouse's education:	5	
Arranged employment bonus:	5	
Maximum	10	
Total	—	—

Fig. 4. Permanent residence assessment chart.

years. Applicants should recognise however, that qualifications for immigration must still be met at the time of initial application. Further information is also available at www.cic.gc.ca the Canadian Government Immigration website.

Provincial immigration programmes

In recent years, emigrating to Canada based on provincial nomination has come into its own. Each province now has a programme, and though each province's programme is unique, they are invariably faster than the 'ordinary' federal system. As the name implies, one must first be nominated by a province to get the benefits of their programme, and there are restrictions in terms of qualifications, the need for a job offer, quotas by province, etc., that must be considered. It should also be noted that nomination by a province usually brings with it the ability to secure a work permit rapidly, so one can be up and running in Canada while their permanent residence application is pending.

Quebec

The most notable of the programmes is Quebec's (though this programme is a selection programme and differs from the others, which are nominee programmes). This is particularly appealing for French-speaking applicants, and the province of Quebec has its own selection criteria. Many investors have also found that the investments available in Quebec provide favourable conditions, and the Quebec investor programme has certainly been one of the more popular programmes. Persons seeking to utilise this system should obtain appropriate counsel and information.

Other programmes

Besides Quebec, and as noted, each province now has its own nominee programme. The details of each programme can be found at each province's website, listed in the 'internet contacts' section, at the end of this book. Full elaboration on each programme is beyond the scope of this book, but a quick summary of each of the programmes, and comparisons, can be found at Figure 5.

FAMILY-BASED IMMIGRATION

In addition to providing assistance in a Skilled Worker application as discussed above, a relative in Canada can help get you to Canada in other ways. While the points provided by a relative in Canada in a Skilled Worker application do not place any obligation on the Canadian resident relative, the situations on page 57 do place an onus on that relative.

Program type available				
Non-business based				
	AB	BC	MN	NFLD	PEI
Employer-driven (application submitted by employer)	Y	Y	Y	N	N
Applicant-driven 'skilled worker'	N	N	Y	Y (job offer required)	Y
International students	N	Y	Y	N	N
Family-based	N	N	Y	N	N
Shortage list-based	Y	Y	Y (see strategic recruitment)	N	N
Others	Low skilled workers	N	Community sponsored; strategic recruitment	N	Connections
Business based				
PNP business program	N	Y	Y	Y	Y
Business case or plan required	N	Y (business skills nominees)	Y	N	Y
Investment (CAD)	N/A	$800,000	$150,000	$200,000	$200,000
Net worth	N	$2M	$250,000	$450,000 (of which $350,000 liquid)	$400,000
Exploratory visit Other requirements	N	Recommended $^{1}/_{3}$ equity in BC business; five new jobs; active management	Y	Y Five years' experience; investment in strategic sector	Y
Prior ownership, business and/or management expertise/ education	N	Y	Y	Y (for senior management)	Y/N
Deposits: refundable and non-refundable	N	N	$75,000	$25,000	$100,000
Alternate business programs	N	Regional business outside major centres; $600,000 net worth, $300,000 investment	Farming business	N	'Partner' ($150,000 investment active role)

Reproduced with the permission of Canada Law Book.

Fig. 5. Provincial Nominee Program Comparison Chart.

Program type available					
Non-business based					
	SK	NB	ON	YK	NS
Employer-driven (application submitted by employer)	N	N	Y	Y	N
Applicant-driven 'skilled worker'	Y (job offer required)	Y (job offer required)	N	Y (job offer required – in specific occupations)	Y (job offer required)
International students	Y	N	Y	N	Y
Family-based	Y	N	N	N	Y
Shortage list-based	N	N	Y	Y (combined with offer above)	
Others	Truckers; health professionals	N	N	N	Community identified
Business based					
PNP business program	Y	Y		Y	Y (criteria being reconsidered)
Business case or plan required	Y	Y		Y	
Investment (CAD)	$150,000	Variable	$10M	$150,000	
Net worth	$250,000	Variable	N/A	$250,000	
Exploratory visit Other requirements	Y	Y Language, active management	N/A Create 25 jobs; allows five nominations	Y Language, primary industries preferred	
Prior ownership, business and/or management expertise/ education	Y	Y	N/A	Y	
Deposits: refundable and non-refundable	$75,000	N	N/A	N	
Alternate business programs	Farmers		N	Self-employed professionals	

Fig. 5. continued.

Sponsorship

Certain family members in Canada can sponsor you. The Canadian relative must be at least 18 years of age and you must be related to them as one of the following:

- father
- mother
- grandfather
- grandmother
- dependent son or daughter (generally under 22, or still in school and financially dependent on the parents)
- spouse, or common-law partner or conjugal partner
- brother, sister, nephew, niece or grandchild who is orphaned, under 19 and unmarried
- adoptive child (meeting certain conditions) (this is now expanded to include guardianships in some cases).

Where a Canadian resident has no relatives in Canada whatsoever, he or she could sponsor you, if you are a more distant relative, even if you are not on the above list.

The Canadian resident will also have to meet certain income requirements. The sponsor must show an income based on the total family size, which includes his or her family members in Canada and you and your accompanying dependants. As always this information can change, and should be checked with a Canadian Visa Post at the time you wish to apply, as well as at an inland Canada Immigration office where your relative will need to make a preliminary application.

The required income starts at $18,371 for one person, and further amounts must be included for each additional person to reach the total income required for a sponsorship. So a Canadian family of four sponsoring a mother would need to show income for five people $38,646, at this time. The information above is just a guideline.

BUSINESS IMMIGRATION

There are three categories of business immigration:

◆ investor
◆ entrepreneur
◆ self-employed.

Investor
An investor is a business person with a net worth of at least $800,000 and who will invest in Canada in a prescribed investment of $400,000. The investment is passive, and is to be repaid, without interest, after five years. In most cases a lump sum (generally in the region of $120,000 to $130,000) can be paid at the outset, without any return, (essentially financing the investment) but sometimes this is actually more cost-effective.

Entrepreneur
An entrepreneur is someone with business experience who intends to be active in a business in Canada, and will have to employ, within three years of arrival, at least one Canadian citizen or permanent resident, essentially start or contribute to a business, and be actively involved in management. You will have to show business experience, and you will need $300,000 net worth to succeed. You will also need to meet the qualifications set out in Figure 4, though the threshold will be different.

Self-employed

A self-employed person is still a business person, but need not employ others. The difference between a self-employed candidate and an entrepreneur is that the self-employed person must show ability to run a business which has some cultural or athletic aspect; for instance a musician, an artist, or some other culturally contributing person.

FEES

Some processing fees relating to Canadian immigration at this time are (in Canadian dollars):

Application for Permanent Residence
    Adult: 550
    Child (up to and including age 21): 150
    Right of Landing Fee (per adult, refundable
    only if refused landing): 490
    Business Application (additional per family): 500
Employment Work Permit: 150

QUALIFYING FOR CITIZENSHIP

This is an area which is set to change in Canadian law. Currently a permanent resident must show three years of residence in the last four, to qualify for Canadian citizenship. Though at this time physical presence is sometimes not required in order to justify 'residence' for citizenship purposes, it is thought that this will soon be changed to require actual physical presence in order to calculate the appropriate time period in Canada. There is also a test of knowledge of basic Canadian issues such as history, politics and language.

BEING REMOVED FROM CANADA

Once you're in Canada, the game is not over. You can still be removed if you violate Canadian immigration law. As noted in some of the sections above, there are various issues which can lead to denial of entry into Canada – those same issues, plus new matters, can also lead to removal once you're here, even if you are a permanent resident.

As with the issues discussed above, criminality is a major concern. Anyone in Canada who is not a citizen and commits a criminal offence is subject to deportation. Permanent residents can sometimes plead to stay on humanitarian grounds (e.g. it was a small matter, an isolated occurrence, I have no family back home, etc.) but the authorities are harsher every day in such cases. In temporary visa situations, overstay is grounds for removal, as is violation of the terms of the stay, such as working while on an ordinary visitor visa.

It is important to be on your best behaviour in order to stay in Canada once here, and to be allowed to return in the future. Deportation, if this is the penalty imposed, is a life-long sentence and can be overcome only with the consent of the Minister of Immigration.

SUMMING UP

The information in this chapter is for general reference only, and not specific legal advice. Each person's case is different and we have tried to give you only a basic understanding of some of the programmes, so that you can see what may be relevant to you. Each programme has much more detail which you can investigate, once you know that you're headed in the right direction. Also, you will certainly need to obtain relevant advice, forms, and guidance to deal with your individual case, which of course will be unique to you. You may wish to begin with a check of www.cic.gac.ca the government's website, previously referenced.

4

Understanding Health and Social Security

The health care system in Canada runs on the principle of universality: every person has free access to basic health care, with a few exceptions. Universal medical coverage was first introduced in Saskatchewan in the early 1960s and the first **Medical Care Act** was legislated in 1968. Doctors bill the public system but they do not work for the government. In fact they are deemed as self-employed and have a great deal of autonomy over how they run their practice (albeit within Canadian guidelines).

There is a lot to be praised about the system, but funding cuts, mismanagement and an ageing population have led to a great deal of upheaval and problems. Every year polls show that health care is the number one concern for Canadians, although recently the environment and climate change has battled health care for the top spot. A few years ago, due to outcries from Canadians and provincial governments, the federal government transferred a lump sum to each province in order to restore health care funding to levels similar to what they were before all the cuts. But with the costs of health care continuing to climb and an ageing population, that money simply kept the system from falling apart.

Compared with many industrialised nations, Canada's health care system is excellent in its standards of care and accessibility. Canadians, for all their complaining about the 'health care crisis' know this and are grateful for all the system offers. But that is not to dismiss their complaints. This chapter is not out to promote the perfection of the Canadian health care system. It is written to provide you with a realistic view of what to expect. Some of the problems being faced are: long waiting lists for elective surgery, delays in cancer treatments due to a shortage of radiologists (in some provinces, for example, patients have been sent to the US so as to not wait a dangerously long time for treatment), shortage of nurses and overcrowded emergency rooms.

Health care falls under provincial jurisdiction but a federal ministry of health ensures that the provinces adhere to the Canada Health Act. Otherwise, provincial and territorial ministries oversee the administration of what is unofficially called **Medicare**.

NUMBER-COUNTING

In 2005, health care spending reached $142 billion, of which just over 70 per cent was public sector spending. The remainder was spent by the private sector (out-of-pocket expenses and third party insurance). For a number of years, private spending was growing at a faster rate than public spending, but it has slowed recently due to an injection of cash from governments. Overall, total health care spending was the equivalent of $4,411 per person.

◆ Most medical expenses are paid for by taxes. Two-thirds of funding comes from general income tax and federal grants through 'block funding' which means the provinces get money based on a per capita basis and can choose to spend it how they like. British Columbia and Alberta do charge premiums, however and Ontario recently brought in a separate health tax.

- There were 63,819 physicians in Canada in 2007. Of those, 32,784 were family physicians and 22,742 were specialists.

- Male doctors outnumber female doctors, but among younger doctors under 35 years of age, there are now more women than there are men.

- In 2005 there were 268,376 registered nurses (RNs) in Canada.

- The majority of doctors are in Ontario with 22,905 physicians, both GPs and specialists. The territories have the least with 130.

- In 2004, Manitoba ranked first and Alberta second for the amount of health care spending per person ($4,465 and $4,316 respectively). Third place went to Ontario ($4,296). The rest of the provinces were as follows: Saskatchewan ($4,145), Newfoundland and Labrador ($4,106), Nova Scotia ($3,974), New Brunswick ($3,968) and PEI ($3,888). Quebec took last place with $3,656. However, the territories, because of their remoteness spend the most per person: Nunavut ($10,411), Northwest Territories ($6,969) and the Yukon ($5,464).

- Life expectancy at birth in Canada is 77.7 for men and 82.5 for women.

PUBLIC VERSUS PRIVATE

Debate rages concerning Canada's health care system and, as some people claim, its increasing Americanisation. Private clinics do exist in Canada and there is the fear that with long waiting lists in the public system, people with money will want to pay for procedures rather than wait, the result being a two-tiered system: one for the rich and one for the poor. With a limited number of specialists in the country, there is also a fear that they'll move to the private clinics and the waiting lists in the public health system will grow longer. But for now, those clinics are funded with public funds and there is officially no queue jumping.

Because it's become clear that the current system is under strain, the Commission on the Future of Health Care in Canada was established, headed by former Saskatchewan premier, Roy Romanow. The Commission's final report on how to sustain the publicly funded system was released in November of 2002 and its recommendations are still being debated five years on.

User fees and extra billing by doctors who also bill the province are not allowed under the **Canada Health Act**. When a person covered by the provincial health plan goes to the doctor, that person does not pay a fee for the visit. The doctor will bill the provincial plan. This pertains to medical doctors only. Psychologists and naturopath doctors, for example, are not covered under provincial plans, chiropractic doctors are only partially covered. Some services from medical doctors, such as medical examinations for summer camp forms or visits to get a medical note for work or school absences, are also not covered and a small fee will be levied.

Things not covered under Canada's Health Act, therefore, have to be provided for with private funds. Prescription and non-prescription drugs, dental services, certain tests, nursing homes and vision care are examples of expenditures people must cover out of their own pockets via direct fees or private insurance. Some provinces partially cover prescription drugs and, for the most part, the government pays for prescriptions for the elderly and people on social assistance.

Going for additional cover

Private insurance plans for individuals and families can be purchased that include a variety of the above, uncovered services. Some of those benefits include: private or semi-private hospital rooms, chiropractic and massage therapy, travel insurance, speech pathology, naturopaths, psychologists, prosthetic appliances etc. Plans vary, but the amount of benefits included is directly related to the cost of the plan. For an individual person, a very basic medical and dental plan can start at around $70 per month. Family plans work out less per person and start at around $140 per month, but for that price very few benefits are included. It is possible that you would be covered by your employer as many companies offer employee benefit packages that include cover for all those things for you, your spouse and your dependent children. A portion of the cost of insurance is often deducted from your pay cheque and the company chips in the rest. If you work for yourself, however, or if you are a contract worker, you will probably have to purchase your own plan. The cost of the plan can be deducted as a medical expense on your income tax return.

KNOWING WHERE TO GO

Hospitals, doctors, walk-in clinics, community health centres and other health care providers are all available. In some provinces, groups of hospitals have merged in attempts to keep costs down. Every major city has several hospitals, smaller cities will have at least one and rural areas usually have a hospital nearby or a clinic within the community. However, rural areas continue to be underserviced despite government incentives to get doctors to set up practices there.

Doctors

Most Canadians choose one family physician to take care of their basic needs. This ensures that the doctor who treats them is someone who knows their medical history. If their medical problem requires a specialist, their doctor will refer them to one.

To choose a doctor you can ask friends, co-workers and family for advice or you can look in the *Yellow Pages* of the telephone book. There are agencies that help immigrants get settled and they too will have a list of available doctors. Doctors limit the number of patients they accept so you may have to look around a bit to find one who is available. The doctor's receptionist can usually tell you of another doctor nearby who is accepting new patients. No one is obliged to remain with a doctor if they are dissatisfied. If you find another doctor you prefer, you can have your records transferred. You are also entitled to a second opinion from another doctor without changing doctors. This is often done if an operation has been recommended or if a serious condition has been diagnosed.

Patients must make an appointment to visit a doctor. A well-organised doctor's office should be able to fit you in on the day you call if it is a serious problem. It is recommended that everyone in the family gets a yearly check-up.

Hospitals

There are over 1,000 hospitals in Canada. Most are general hospitals, but a small percentage are convalescent or chronic care hospitals. Ninety-five per cent of hospitals are private, not-for-profit corporations. The administrators who manage them report to hospital boards made up of public trustees. Clinical staff makes the medical decisions, however.

Hospital emergency rooms have been strained under cuts to funding. Some emergency doctors complain that the emergency rooms are overcrowded because people come in with trivial problems, especially as many people are without a family doctor. Both rural and urban areas are experiencing a shortage of family physicians (and specialists) so it's likely both a shortage in funding and non-emergencies have led to the problem of long emergency room waits.

In the case of an emergency, an ambulance would take you to the nearest and least busy hospital emergency room. If you are scheduled to go to the hospital for any reason, you may be slated to go to a hospital at which your family doctor has hospital privileges unless you are going in for a service available at only certain hospitals or for surgery. Where you go for surgery depends on the surgeon involved.

If a life is in danger, there is an emergency telephone number to call; in most cities that number is 911. This will get you ambulance, fire or police services immediately. In other communities you can call the operator by dialling 0. If the doctor determines you did not need the ambulance, you will be required to pay for it. In some provinces, part of the ambulance fee must be paid even if the ambulance was required, although some private insurance plans cover this fee.

Clinics

For visitors, people without a family doctor or for after-hours care, an alternative to hospital emergency rooms is a walk-in clinic. Some are small, staffed by one or two doctors, while others are comprehensive clinics with their own specialists. They are not 24-hour care facilities but the hours are longer than those of a regular doctor's office. If you need more serious care or X-rays, the clinic may send you to a nearby diagnostic centre where they specialise in X-rays, ultrasound and lab work. These are privately run, but if you're covered by provincial health care the tests will be covered. The clinic may also send you to a hospital emergency room.

CONTROLLING DISEASE

Canada's public health laws protect its people in various ways. One of those measures is compulsory vaccination to inoculate against certain diseases. Polio, diphtheria, mumps, measles and chicken pox have been eliminated or reduced because of high public health standards. It is the law that children must be immunised against serious infectious diseases such as diphtheria, polio and tetanus. Children are not allowed to go to school without an immunisation card to prove their vaccinations are up to date. Inoculations can be arranged through a doctor or public health clinic.

In 2006, Health Canada approved the vaccine to protect girls from the human papilloma virus (HPV), which is responsible for most cases of cervical cancer. Nova Scotia became the first province to announce it would have a programme to inoculate girls in grade 7, although the vaccinations won't be mandatory. Other provinces will monitor Nova Scotia's efforts to see if they want to adopt similar programmes.

Some high schools and most universities have included condom machines in the student washrooms. This is a measure to try to control sexually transmitted diseases.

ELIGIBILITY AND THE HEALTH CARD

Provincial health insurance plans cover essential medical services for all Canadian citizens and permanent residents. Visitors must have travel health insurance. Visitors in Canada on a working permit may be covered by a provincial plan, but this depends on the province, the job and the length of contract. In Quebec, for example, workers from France with contracts for more than three months are eligible for coverage for the time of their contracts. Quebec also has agreements with citizens of Sweden, Finland, Norway, Denmark, Portugal and Luxembourg. Quebec does not have an agreement with the United Kingdom. It is important, as a worker, that you check with the province you will be working in as to what their rules are. Moreover, even if you are covered, there may be a waiting period before you are entitled to the coverage. For student coverage, see Chapter 8.

Obtaining a health card

If you are eligible, you must obtain a **health card**. Each province has its own particular requirements. When you arrive you must apply right away for a health card at the province's ministry of health in your city. When you apply you must bring with you your birth certificate, your immigration visa and passport. Some provinces also require documentation showing your name and address and your signature. Every member of your family must get a health card.

In most provinces you will be eligible right away, but in British Columbia, Ontario and New Brunswick there is a three-month waiting period. Temporary workers may face different waiting periods in those and the other provinces. For the time that you as a worker are not covered, you should buy cover through a private insurance plan, such as travel insurance from your home country.

If you move to another province, you may face a waiting period before being eligible for the health plan in that new province, so you should apply right away. In the meantime you will be covered by the plan of the province you just left. If you are simply visiting another province, your card can be used in an emergency.

LOOKING AT THE DETAILS

Medicines

Prescription drugs are strictly controlled in Canada. There are many examples of drugs that are available over the counter in Europe and America but that are available only by prescription in Canada. Most drugs for minor maladies such as headaches, colds and sore throats are available in the aisles of the pharmacies. When you need something more serious, your doctor will write a prescription for you which you take to the pharmacist to get filled. Prescription drugs can be quite costly, which is why most people get private insurance, which covers all or part of the drug costs (employer plans do this too). Herbal medicines are available over the counter in both mainstream drug stores as well as natural/health food stores, although new regulations on them are near to being on the books.

Dental services

Unfortunately, dental services are not covered under provincial health plans. You can get cover through your company's benefit package (if available) or through a private insurance plan that also covers prescription drugs. If not, you can pay as you go. It is recommended that people, including children, get a check-up and cleaning twice a year and X-rays every few years (to identify cavities and structural problems). A cleaning and check-up can cost from $60 to $95. Filling cavities can cost hundreds of dollars, which is why it is cheaper to have regular check-ups and catch problems before they become serious. Teeth, their health and their appearance, are a high priority for Canadians. It is very common for teenagers to undergo orthodontic work to straighten teeth and bites. Orthodontic work is very expensive, however.

Pregnancy

Most women choose to have their babies in a hospital, but home births with a midwife are gaining popularity. Pregnancy is taken seriously in Canada and the standard of care is excellent. In addition to a family doctor monitoring a pregnant patient, the prospective mother will likely solicit the services of an obstetrician/gynaecologist, even if the pregnancy appears to be normal. Hospitals and clinics offer childbirth and child care courses.

Abortion is a very controversial subject in Canada, as it is elsewhere in the world. Demonstrations and serious violence have shown that. Regardless, you should know that abortion is not illegal in Canada, although it is not available at all health care facilities.

Accountability

Provincial colleges of physicians and surgeons regulate doctors and handle complaints about doctors. But, there are also complaints about the colleges for being inefficient and protective of doctors. Despite this, the colleges remain the only real mechanism for accountability. Although a new and controversial website www.ratemds.com has sprung up allowing patients to write online about their experiences with a doctor. Otherwise the only other option is through legal means, in terms of malpractice lawsuits, which are also cumbersome and fairly expensive.

SOCIAL SECURITY

Old age pensions, family allowance, unemployment insurance and welfare are just some of the programmes in Canada's extensive social security network. Specific circumstances must be met in order to qualify for each type of government assistance, such as having worked a required amount of time leading up to the benefit. Other benefits require that you have paid into them to be eligible to receive them. A person may qualify for more than one programme, but each must be applied for separately. To qualify for any of the benefits a **Social Insurance Number** is required. See Chapter 7 for more information on how to get a **SIN**.

Old Age Security

An **Old Age Security (OAS)** pension is for people over the age of 65. A Canadian citizen or permanent resident who has lived in Canada for 40 years after the age of 18 is eligible for a full OAS pension. Seniors who have lived in Canada for less than 40 years may receive a reduced pension. Permanent residents from some countries may be able to get old age security from their original country.

Pensioners with little or no other income may be eligible for the **Guaranteed Income Supplement (GIS)**. If between 60 and 64, the spouse of a low income or deceased pensioner may qualify for the **Spouse's Allowance (SPA)**. GIS and SPA are available to pensioners who can prove they are in need of the money. Pensioners have to apply for these two benefits, as they don't kick in automatically even if your income tax return indicates you are below a certain income. In other words, the government won't tell you if you're eligible. It's up to you to find out.

Canada and Quebec pension plans

To qualify for these, people must have contributed to the plan during their working years. Usually an amount is automatically deducted from one's pay cheque. Eligibility is extended to Canadian citizens, permanent residents, visitors and holders of a Minister's Permit who have been in Canada for one year and whose income during that year was subject to Canadian income tax and CPP/QPP deductions. Monthly payments begin at 65 years of age (a reduced pension is available at age 60) and the amount paid depends on the amount contributed. Spouses of deceased pensioners are entitled to survivors' pensions.

Included in these plans are disability pensions – both for short-term and long-term disability. As well there are benefits for dependent children of disabled parents and death benefits for children whose parent(s) have died.

Child tax benefits

The **Canada Child Tax Benefit** (CCTB) is made in monthly payments to parents or guardians on behalf of a child under the age of 18. The amount varies according to family income, number of children and their ages. To qualify, you must be the parent or guardian of the child who lives with you. You or your spouse must be either a Canadian citizen, permanent resident, visitor or holder of a Minister's Permit who has lived in Canada for at least 18 consecutive months before applying for the benefit.

The CCTB may include the **National Child Benefit Supplement** (for low-income families) and the **Child Disability Benefit**. Several provinces and the territories have supplemental child tax credit programmes as well.

The federal government recently introduced the **Universal Child Care Benefit** (UCCB). It is for children under six years of age and is paid in monthly instalments of $100 per child. You must apply for it; the benefit is not automatic.

Employment Insurance

The government has recently renamed unemployment insurance, **Employment Insurance**. This has brought on a smidgen of ridicule, as some believe this was to soften the negative connotations of the word 'unemployment'. Most people still refer to it as 'unemployment insurance in conversation'. Regardless of what you call it, this is how it works. Payments to Employment Insurance (EI) are made through deductions from a person's pay cheque. To qualify, a person has to have worked for a minimum amount of time (required amount of time depends on where you live and the unemployment rate in that region) and has to have lost his or her job through no fault of their own. For example if the reason for unemployment is the birth or adoption of a child, enrolment in a national training programme, work sharing or job training, a person may be eligible. As well, if a person is laid off from a job through company restructuring or due to bankruptcy, a person will usually qualify. After a certain period of time, if a person has not been able to find a job, EI benefits cease and the person must apply for Social Assistance.

Employment Insurance also covers maternity leave. Maternity benefits are payable to the mother for a maximum of 15 weeks (although she can take 17 weeks off) as long as she worked for 600 hours in the last year. There is also parental leave for up to 35 weeks. A mother can add that to her maternity leave, share it with the father, or the father can take all 35 weeks. Parental leave is also available to adoptive parents. Some employers 'top up' your income for a number of weeks, but don't count on it. However, employers are obliged to keep your job for you regardless of whether you take the 17 weeks or a full year. Quebec has its own maternity and paternal leave programme that is, in some ways, more generous than the federal programme.

Social Assistance
Often called 'welfare', this benefit is solely for people in need who are not eligible for other benefits. Payments are to help pay for necessities such as food, shelter, clothing, prescription drugs and

other health services. Local offices of the provincial or municipal departments of social services usually oversee and administer Social Assistance. The size of payment varies from region to region, as do eligibility rules. In some cases there is the ability to join programmes to train for available work.

Workers' Compensation

If you get injured at work you may qualify for financial benefits and medical and rehabilitative services. You must prove your injury was work-related and offer medical reports for assessment. The decision regarding your eligibility rests with the provincial workers' compensation board offices. In Ontario that board is named the Workplace Safety and Insurance Board, rather than the Workers' Compensation Board as in other provinces.

Applying for social security programmes

Except for workers' compensation and child tax benefits, benefits are applied for through Service Canada. There are branches in all cities. You will need a birth or baptismal certificate, passport and a Canada Immigration visa. For the child tax benefit you need to apply to Revenue Canada, Taxation. Again, an immigration visa needs to be provided as does proof of birth for each child.

Taxation

Canadians are a relatively highly taxed bunch. It simply goes with providing a social security net. Someone has to pay for all the government programmes people need and enjoy. Even though Canadians recognise the need for taxes, it is a sore spot for many who feel the tax system takes too much out of the pockets of hard-working individuals. You'll find promises of tax cuts usually surface during any election. Because of that, the information in this chapter is a rough guide only. Taxation rates, laws and rules change all the time – even accountants have a hard time keeping up.

INCOME TAX

Personal income tax is the portion of money people pay out of their earnings – from working, from investments, or from renting their property out to others – to the government. It was first employed in 1917 to help pay the war debt. It was meant to be a temporary measure until the debt was paid off, but it has never been discontinued and it now accounts for a large portion of government revenue.

Canada's income tax system is 'progressive' in that it requires people who make more money to pay a larger percentage of their income in tax. Tax is paid on an individual's taxable income, which is that person's income after deductions, such as valid medical expenses, moving expenses, charitable donations, tuition, **Registered Retirement Saving Plan** (RRSP) contributions, etc.

An RRSP is a retirement plan that you register with the federal government. Many people do so through a private investment firm or financial institution, often investing in mutual funds, stocks, and money markets. For some people the amount they squirrel away in an RRSP will be their entire pension; for others it is in addition to a pension being built through their employer. Each year you have a limit of what you can contribute to your RRSP based on your income, and those contributions are tax deductible, thereby reducing your income tax.

Any income you earn in the RRSP is usually exempt from tax for the time the funds remain in the plan. You pay the tax when you cash it in or make withdrawals (usually upon retirement). The thinking is that when you retire, your income will be less and therefore your tax bracket lower so that you end up paying less tax overall.

Federal Taxation Rates

Taxable income	Rate
$37,178.00 or less*	15.5%
$37,178.01 – $74,357.00	22%
$74,357.01 – $120,887.00	26%
$120,887.01 or more	29%

In 2007, Canadians could claim a basic amount of $8,929 before being taxed.

It may seem strange that there is only a 3 per cent difference between the middle range and the highest range and this has been a source of contention in political debates as many see it as unfair to the middle classes. There are also many political arguments regarding the scope of the tax brackets. Why is someone who makes $38,000 in the same bracket as someone making almost $74,000?

In addition to these basic rates there is a federal surtax, provincial taxes (which vary from province to province, but except in Quebec are calculated by the same federal Tax On Income or – TONI – method; in Quebec it's calculated as a percentage of the federal tax payable) and provincial surtaxes. The combined effect of this can see the people in the top bracket paying more than half of their income to the government. If you run your own business or are a contract worker, you set up your own payment plan with the government. This usually means making quarterly payments to Revenue Canada.

During the year, your employer will automatically deduct income tax from your pay cheque by an amount corresponding to your tax bracket. Even so, every year you must file a tax return claiming your income and deductions. When you start work with an employer you will fill out a form that will determine how much tax is taken off your pay cheque. That form, the T1, can indicate that although you earn X amount per year, less tax should be taken off because you will have deductions like tuition, RRSP contributions or a dependant (such as a child or ill parent). At the same time, you could also indicate that more tax should be taken off than would normally for your annual income. This would be done in the case where you know you have other sources of income that will add to your taxable income.

Depending on whether you have overpaid or underpaid through payroll deductions, the result of your tax return will mean either you are entitled to a refund of what you overpaid or you owe a balance to the government.

Foreign income, income you earn through business, overseas investments, etc., is not exempt.

GOODS AND SERVICES TAX

The **Goods and Services Tax (GST)** was implemented on 1 January 1991. It is a general sales tax that applies to the sale of most goods and services. It was brought in to replace existing 'hidden' manufacturing taxes. The GST was recently reduced from 7 to 6 per cent. It is charged at the time of purchase. Its proposal and eventual implementation raised a huge political debate and although subsequent governments promised to remove it, they found they could not afford to because, like income tax, it has become an important source of revenue.

When you buy goods, the price on the tag is the price before either the sales tax (see below) or the GST. So, for instance, if you are buying a magazine for $3 in Ontario and you go to the cash register, the price that will ring up is $3.42. In other words, you pay $3 plus 14 per cent (6 per cent GST and Ontario has a 8 per cent provincial sales tax).

If a person's income is deemed low enough, he or she may be eligible for a GST credit, something a person applies for on his or her income tax return. If you are just visiting Canada as a tourist, you can apply for a GST refund for purchases over $50.

PROVINCIAL SALES TAX/HARMONISED SALES TAX

All the provinces have a sales tax that you pay on goods that you purchase, or have a harmonised sales tax that combines the GST and retail tax into one. Alberta is the exception – it has only the national GST. Rates vary from province to province as do which goods are exempted from sales tax (see Figure 6).

Province	GST/HST		PST	Combined rate
British Columbia	6%	GST	7%	13.8%
Alberta	6%	GST	0%	6%
Saskatchewan	6%	GST	7%	13%
Manitoba	6%	GST	7%	13%
Ontario	6%	GST	8%	14%
Quebec	6%	GST	7.5%	13.95%*
Newfoundland & Labrador	14%	HST	n/a	14%
Nova Scotia	14%	HST	n/a	14%
New Brunswick	14%	HST	n/a	14%
Prince Edward Island	6%	GST	10%	16.7%*
Yukon Territory	6%	GST	0%	6%
North West Territories	6%	GST	0%	6%
Nunavut	6%	GST	0%	6%

In Quebec and Prince Edward Island only, the GST is included in the provincial sales tax base.

Fig. 6. Provincial sales tax rates.

PROPERTY TAXES

Property taxes are municipalities' principal income other than user fees (water, transit etc.), fines, permit fees, investment income and transfer payments from the province. These taxes are based on the value of land and buildings that you own (e.g. your house, business building etc.). In major cities, the rates can translate into a couple of thousand dollars a year and upwards on a house. The money goes to such essential services as snow removal, garbage removal, public transport etc. It is an annual tax.

CORPORATE TAXES

Corporations pay a corporate income tax on the income they earn. The federal government is lowering those taxes, as it is with personal income taxes, over the next few years. Currently, the combined rate (federal and provincial) is about 30 per cent, depending on the province. For Canadian-controlled private corporations that can claim a small business deduction, the tax rate works out to be 12 per cent.

Those rates may be further reduced through incentive provisions and tax breaks that encourage businesses to stay in Canada.

One problem for Canada has been that it has higher corporate taxation rates than the United States and Mexico with whom Canada has a free trade agreement. One of the reasons for the government's goal of lowering corporate taxes is that over the years, some industries have moved south where the tax and labour costs are lower, which has meant some Canadian job losses.

OTHER TAXES

- **Tariffs or duties**: taxes on the value of goods entering or leaving Canada. They are used to protect Canadian industry from foreign competition.
- **Excise taxes**: sales taxes that are imposed on the sale of a specific item.
- **Luxury tax**: an excise tax on a good considered to be a luxury.
- **Estate taxes**: arise when the government takes a portion of the wealth of a person who has died.

♦ **Inheritance taxes**: when an individual receives something from a person who has died, that individual must pay part of the inheritance to the government.

SEEING WHERE IT ALL GOES

Taxes pay for social programmes, public works, education (all levels), health care and more. Unfortunately, because of the large debt Canada has accrued, Canadians' tax dollars also go to paying the interest payments on that debt rather than going directly to fund programmes.

The federal government collects federal income tax and also collects the provincial income tax on behalf of the provinces through an agreement it has with the provinces. The provincial governments' revenues come from such taxes as well as from transfer payments for the federal government. This is partly due to the fact that the provinces have some of the costliest responsibilities: health and education. And, as mentioned before, the federal government also doles out equalisation payments to the less prosperous provinces.

Most municipalities receive some sort of transfer payment from their respective provincial governments or operate programmes on a cost sharing basis with the province. This is because municipalities have limited sources of revenue, which is a constant source of friction between the cities and the other levels of government, especially when the federal government continues to pull in billions of dollars in surpluses due to gas taxes and employment insurance premiums. For several years, the cities got little in return; there had been minimal help for cities to deal with roads, public transportation and housing. But in the last few years, the federal government has begun to dedicate funds to those kinds of needs. They've done that through giving a portion of the gas tax back to municipalities and through special targeted infrastructure programmes. Some provinces have followed suit.

TIPPING

This is not really a tax, but you should know that tipping is customary in Canada. It is predominantly supposed to reward good service, but people often feel compelled to tip because they think it's expected. If you do tip, 15 per cent (before tax) is the usual amount for such service providers as waitresses, bartenders, taxi drivers, hairdressers and chambermaids (hotels). The choice is yours, of course, but keep in mind that jobs like waitressing and bartending make lower wages because it is expected that people in those positions will make it up in tips.

Finding a Place to Live

Finding a place you can call home will probably be one of the most important decisions that you make when coming to Canada. Whether you're coming to work for a short period of time or to live permanently, the place you trudge 'home' to every night will make a big difference to how you adjust to your new life. However, most newcomers do not start out in a palace and should not worry if they are not all that keen on their first apartment. In fact, moving might be the first very Canadian thing they do. One out of every two Canadians moves every three years. And in 2005, the average household spent $12,610 on shelter.

There are numerous factors to take into account when choosing the place you want to call home. Renting or owning, location and cost will probably be the most important factors.

ASSESSING HOUSEHOLD CHARACTERISTICS

In 2002 the average number of people in a household was 2.5 and the average rooms per dwelling was 6.1. Because Canada has some fairly bitter winters, most houses and apartments have insulated walls, double windows and central heating. Most homes are heated by a hot air furnace or electric heating. The principal heating fuel is piped gas and electricity and the majority of households cook with electricity. According to the latest figures, almost 24 per cent of households have more than one refrigerator,

38 per cent of households have air conditioners and 42 per cent have three or more telephones and 52 per cent have cellular telephones.

RENTING

Renting an apartment, house or part of a house is how most people start out. The typical apartment is a self-contained unit in a multi-floor building, but many houses have been converted into rental units so a tenant may rent the first or second floor of a house, each floor being its own self-contained unit. These are usually called 'flats'. You can also rent an entire house or a room in a house (the latter is called 'shared accommodation'). It's hard to say when is the best time to look for accommodation, because it depends on the city. In university towns, a large number of students will be looking for leases that start in the autumn, so it's best to avoid that time. In major cities, spring, summer and autumn are all good times to look. Good bargains can be found in the winter, but it's not fun to move in that season and there's less to choose from. When looking for a lease, start a month or two before you want to begin renting, as listings don't usually come up more than a month or two in advance. Be aware that while in some cities, vacancy rates have risen a bit (as people choose to buy instead of rent), in other cities the market is still tipped in the landlord's/owner's favour with rates barely above one per cent.

Choosing the type of dwelling

One of the cheapest options is to rent a room in a shared house. Many students and single people do this when they are starting out. Bachelor apartments consist of one main room with a kitchen, sleeping area and a separate bathroom. They are designed mainly for one person, two at the most. After that there are one-, two- and three-bedroom apartments. Some are even larger than that. Then there are penthouse or loft-types that fall under the category of 'luxury apartments'. Furnished apartments and rooms can also be rented.

Counting the cost

Rental costs vary widely from city to city. Prices tend to be much, much higher in urban areas, especially cities like Vancouver and Toronto. It is very difficult to give general estimates because prices within a city vary as well, with downtown prices being far costlier than outlying neighbourhoods. In Toronto, for example, you could be looking at $800 per month for a bachelor apartment and $1,100 for a one-bedroom, but those prices could be less or more depending on the neighbourhood. In a smaller city or town, prices are usually a few hundred dollars less. For instance, in Saskatoon you could get a one-bedroom for around $400. Each province also has rules on how much a landlord can increase the rent each year for an existing or new tenant. Disputes between tenants and landlords can be taken to the appropriate rental authority or tribunal.

It is important to note that rent paid may or may not include such utilities as heat, electricity, gas and water. Before you agree to a rent, find out what it includes. Cable for television and the cost of a telephone line are usually not included and you will be billed directly by the respective utility companies for those amenities.

The landlord pays the property taxes and takes care of insurance for the building, but the tenant is responsible for insuring individual personal items.

What comes with an apartment?

Every apartment should have its own private entrance (off the street or a common hallway) through a door that can be locked. It should have a kitchen with a sink and tap supplying both cold and hot water, and a bathroom with a sink, toilet and a bath or shower. Appliances such as a stove and refrigerator should also be included. The apartment should be equipped with light and electricity, sewage pipes, telephone lines (you will have to pay for hook-up) and, of course, a heating system. Optional facilities that might make a place more enticing are laundry and parking facilities.

The landlord is responsible for maintenance of the unit. If things like an appliance that came with the apartment, a door or a roof are broken, you can call the landlord to arrange to get a repair person in to fix it. Unless you are responsible for the breakage, the landlord also absorbs the cost.

Taking steps to find an apartment

The best places to look are in the classified advertisements in local newspapers or online. Your friends, co-workers and family may hear something by word-of-mouth that may be a lead to a place not listed. In the bigger cities some people even hire real estate agents to find rental units, but doing so is by no means necessary. The other method is to drive around prospective neighbourhoods and look for signs saying, for rent or for lease.

It is wise to be selective and to look at a few places before deciding. The risk, in competitive markets like Vancouver, Calgary, Toronto and Ottawa, is that in the meantime someone else gets the apartment. In fact, for some types of markets you're likely to have to fill out an application to be compared with other would-be renters. When you go to see the apartment, make sure you look neat and clean and be at your friendliest. Making a good impression in person can go a long way to furthering your paper application. Find out when the landlord plans to make a decision and if you don't get a call by then, check back. Some landlords don't want tenants with pets or tenants who smoke. In some provinces it's against the law to refuse a person an apartment based on that. But it's hard to prove that you lost out on an apartment because you had a pet or you're a smoker.

Factors you should consider when deciding on a place are nearby public transport (especially if you do not have a car), conveniently located shops, parking and schools. If these things are in order and you like the size, price range (find out how much utilities cost the last tenant) and neighbourhood, you are probably making a good decision.

Following the right procedure
It is proper procedure to telephone to make an appointment to see an apartment. If you decide you want it and the landlord accepts you as a tenant, you will probably be asked for the first and last month's rent as a deposit except in Quebec where they're not allowed to ask for last month's rent. Whenever you move on, that last month's rent will be applied to your last month, saving you the cheque at that time. In some provinces, the landlord must also pay you a certain percentage interest on that last month's rent deposit.

The next step is for you and the landlord to sign a rental agreement or lease. Most landlords will ask you to sign for a year's lease. But month-to-month and other rental periods are allowed. Make sure you make note of any damage at the start and point it out to the landlord so as to not be blamed for it yourself.

In most cases, the landlord will do a credit check to ensure that you have enough money to pay rent and that you have a good credit rating.

Renting other properties
Renting a house is a similar process to renting an apartment, you just end up with more space and appliances.

To rent a condo apartment you will most likely need to enlist the help of a real estate agent. Rent is paid to the owners of the condo not to the building's management.

Renting an apartment in a co-op building means you are also responsible for some task in the maintenance or running of the building.

OWNING

Owning a house or condominium is a big deal. It is a huge responsibility, both financially and practically. Like a renter, a buyer should take into account many factors when looking to purchase property. But unlike a renter who can move easily, factors like location and condition of the property are extremely important. After all, you will probably be in that house for a long time.

Buying a house
The best time to look is spring and early summer. The real estate

markets for houses vary greatly from city to city. The bigger the city, generally, the more expensive the real estate. Figure 7 lists average house prices west to east.

The average price of a house, nationally, has for the first time ever nudged above $300,000. However, before you panic at that amount, consider the economic boom in the west, specifically in Alberta. The increase in house prices there account, in large part, for the growing national price.

And, as you can see, Montreal prices are lower than Toronto. During years of political instability, many people left the province which resulted in a real estate slump. However, as the issue of separation has moved to the backburner, the prices in Montreal have started to pick up.

House prices reflect the demand for housing, which is why it costs more to live in a large city. People flock to cities to find jobs, especially with higher wages.

How to buy a house

Again, the best sources for information will be classified ads (whether online or in newspapers), real estate agencies, friends and neighbours. See Useful Addresses (page 209) for a list of newspapers in which you can search the classifieds on their websites.

In an attempt to avoid fees and commissions some people try to do private sales, but the majority of buying and selling is done through real estate agencies. Most buyers obtain pre-approval for

City	Province	Average price ($)
Victoria	British Columbia	429,426*
Vancouver	British Columbia	564,702
Edmonton	Alberta	350,357
Calgary	Alberta	427,205
Regina	Saskatchewan	169,729
Saskatoon	Saskatchewan	252,444
Winnipeg	Manitoba	185,447
Thunder Bay	Ontario	120,150
Sudbury	Ontario	184,986
Windsor	Ontario	164,317
London	Ontario	204,500
Kitchener	Ontario	256,588
St. Catharines & District	Ontario	219,857
Hamilton – Burlington & District	Ontario	269,676
Toronto	Ontario	381,963
Ottawa	Ontario/Quebec	279,361
Montreal	Quebec	235,087
Quebec City	Quebec	164,298
Saint John	New Brunswick	144,769
Halifax – Dartmouth	Nova Scotia	225,467
St. John's	Newfoundland & Labrador	141,632*

Based on June 2007 figures from the Canadian Real Estate Association (not seasonally adjusted)
* December 2006

Fig. 7. Average house prices.

a mortgage first (see mortgages section below) so that sellers and real estate agents know the buyer is serious and know how much the buyer has to spend.

A real estate agent will show you several houses based on what you have stated to be your price range, desired type of neighbourhood and taste in architecture. Once you decide on a house, you normally make a legal written offer (this includes the deposit) on the condition that the house passes an official inspection of its condition and structure. Usually you will negotiate (in writing) with the seller to get the best price you can and once the seller accepts an offer it becomes an agreement to purchase.

Mortgages

Unless you have money to burn, you will probably need to set up a mortgage with a bank or trust company. First you will have to pay a deposit that is ordinarily around 20–25 per cent of the total price. If you are a first-time homebuyer you may qualify for a smaller down-payment of 5–10 per cent. The rest of the purchase is paid in monthly payments including interest. If you put down less than 25 per cent, you have to take out mortgage insurance through your lender, which gets it from the Canada Home Mortgage Corporation. In fact, the CHMC has a programme through which you can put down as little as 5 per cent, but there are limits on the price of the house you wish to buy if you put down 10 per cent or less.

The federal government also has a programme for first-time home buyers whereby they can withdraw up to $20,000 from their RRSP (Registered Retirement Savings Plan) towards the cost of building or buying a home. That amount gets paid back into the RRSP, interest free, but has to be repaid within 15 years. Any balance remaining is deemed income and taxable in the 16th year. However, if you are new to Canada you won't be likely to have an RRSP yet. At the same time, you might not plan to buy for a few years (and rent in the meantime); you could take that time to start investing in an RRSP so that when you are ready to buy you have that option to borrow from it.

Mortgages usually come with a fixed interest rate for a term of one to five years, but there are an increasing number of options including variable rate mortgages. The shorter the term agreed upon, the lower the interest rate, but the greater the uncertainty is regarding future interest rates on agreement renewals. Many buyers look for clauses that allow them at certain times to put more money towards the principal and therefore pay off their mortgage sooner. On average, most buyers pay for their houses over 15 to 25 years.

What you own

If you hold a freehold estate, you own both the house and the land that it sits upon and only the government has rights to interfere with the land (it must give notice, of course). Most ownership in Canada is freehold. If you own a leasehold estate you own the house but not the land.

Other costs

Your home will have been assessed for property taxes, which you have to pay every year. Such taxes vary from region to region, from property to property. Larger properties have higher property taxes, as do properties occupying corner lots.

As an owner, you are also responsible for the maintenance of the house and appliances within the house. Whether it is a clogged drain, a leaky pipe or a leaky roof, you have to organise and pay for the repairs. There will also be utility costs, such as hydroelectricity, heat and water.

Buying a condominium

These are individually owned apartments or townhouses (terraced houses) where common areas (gardens, pools, walkways, etc.) are owned together. On top of your mortgage payments and your property taxes, a condominium fee is levied to cover maintenance and repairs by the management of the condominium.

The condominium is usually managed by a condo board made up of people who live in the building or property (i.e. your neighbours). Condo fees can be a few hundred dollars a month or more. Condos are often more affordable than houses, but you often get less square footage for the money you're paying. But there is the convenience of not having to mow the grass or shovel the snow.

DISCRIMINATION

The **Canadian Charter of Rights and Freedoms** protects prospective renters and buyers from discrimination based on a whole host of factors such as gender, race and religion. That means a landlord or seller cannot refuse to rent or sell to you based on such factors. However, this is not to say it does not happen. If you feel you have been unfairly discriminated against you can contact the **Human Rights Commission** in your province.

GOVERNMENT-SUBSIDISED HOUSING

In most cities there is special housing for people with low incomes or special needs. Through the 1990s, governments said they will not 'be in the housing business' and, therefore, the existing stock had not been added to for years. However, recognising there is a lack of affordable housing, the federal government recently initiated a programme with the provinces and cities to build some affordable housing units. The programme has funds of hundreds of millions of dollars, but even that will see some cities get at most only 1,000 new units, when there are thousands of people and families on the waiting lists.

You may know such housing as 'social housing' or 'council housing' in the country from which you came. You may, however, be quite surprised at the differences between such housing in Canada and that in your former country.

Subsidised housing usually comes in the form of apartment buildings, not houses, therefore there is no option to buy. To avoid the creation of ghettos, most subsidised housing was not built all in one area, but was scattered throughout city neighbourhoods. However, that's not to say ghettos don't exist, especially since some buildings are clustered together all in one area. Some buildings have units that are rented at a normal rate for those who can afford it, while other units in the building are rented at rates geared to a tenant's income. There is also special housing for the disabled and the elderly that is income-geared. But as mentioned, demand far outstrips supply and there are some fairly lengthy waiting lists for such housing, some as long as seven or more years.

OBTAINING TELEPHONE, CABLE AND THE INTERNET

Getting hooked up

Once you know where you will be living, you need to get in touch the telephone company and have them hook up the line that probably already exists in your new home. They do not need to come to your place to do this, unless no line exists or you want more telephone sockets or more than one line put in. The local telephone company has a huge assortment of options for phone service, and you can either rent or buy a phone from the company, or you can buy one from an electronics store. The hook-up costs a one-time fee, and the line is paid for monthly and ranges in price from city to city. The monthly fee can cost anything from $20–$35 with no additional features (such as an internal answering machine, call waiting and call display). It includes all local calls. You can choose a local phone company to be your long distance carrier but you can choose to have one company provide your local service and another to be your long-distance carrier. It pays to shop around.

Cable TV

Getting cable for your television works much the same way, with a one-time hook-up fee (per television set). Various packages exist that range in price, and the number of channels received is directly proportional to the price paid per month. You can receive about three channels without basic cable if you have a television set with a good pair of 'rabbit ears' (antennae). Basic cable can cost from $17 to $25 per month depending on the city. Extended cable is available for around $40 a month, which gives approximately 50–60 channels. Of course, many of these channels carry programmes you couldn't care less to watch.

Digital TV

Digital television is another option, which you can get either through a satellite or cable company. Digital is more expensive than basic cable and there are compatibility issues with regards to what kind of television set you have and in the case of digital through satellite, whether you can put a satellite dish on your roof or balcony (sometimes not allowed in apartment buildings or multi-unit houses). The benefits are that you'll see a better quality picture and have a greater selection of channels. Also digital providers have special features they offer, such as films on demand and personal video recorders (PVRs). PVRs allow the recording of television programmes onto a hard drive.

Joining the Internet

Internet service can be acquired through telephone lines or through cable. Telephone companies, cable companies and local Internet service providers (ISPs) offer various packages and, again, it pays to shop around. Telephone companies and ISPs offer both dial-up and high-speed service. Cable companies only offer high-speed service. High speed is clearly much faster than dial-up, but also more expensive, ranging from $35 to $50 per month, which does not include hook-up and set-up costs, although high speed comes with unlimited hours online. Dial-up ranges from $10 to $25 per month, depending on the number of hours you sign up for.

CONSIDERING SAFETY

It is not much good to live in a place you like and yet not feel safe. Your home should have smoke and carbon monoxide detectors. If you rent your abode, the installation of such devices is the responsibility of the landlord. You should also have fire extinguishers placed around the house. Canadian cities are very safe and the crime rate is actually declining, but it is still a good idea to lock doors and windows.

In recent years there have been a number of tragedies where young children have fallen out of windows from the upper levels of a house or a high rise building. Make sure your windows have screens and that those screens are securely fastened, and that there is no easy way for a young child to climb up on furniture near a window. If you have a balcony, make sure you supervise your children if they go on it.

OBTAINING HOUSEHOLD GOODS

Bring or buy?

First consider the electrical compatibility of your country with Canada. Canada operates on 110-V, 60-cycle electric power. Hairdryers and razors often have dual-voltage capability, but appliances like televisions, stereos and microwaves do not. If your country uses a higher voltage, you could buy a transformer for each appliance as well as a plug adapter. But sometimes even that won't solve the problem and the appliance (especially VCRs – in Canada the system used is VHS, not PAL which is used in the UK) is impossible to use. DVD players as well, are not compatible with all DVD discs. In fact the discs and players are coded for a region, of which six exist in the world. Therefore, a disc coded for region one cannot be played in a DVD player coded for region three. Canada is region one and shares that coding with the US only. Europe is region two. There are DVD players that will initially play all types of discs, but after a few times they will ask you to permanently choose a disc code.

Adapting, transforming and shipping costs may total more than the cost of buying a new appliance in Canada. Figure 8 gives a list of prices of a sampling of Canadian goods, if bought new. There are also stores that sell used consumer goods.

There is a great deal of choice in Canada. There are stores that specialise in bulk or discount prices while others cater only to the top of the market, and there is more selection in major cities than in rural centres. In the north, prices are usually higher.

You're allowed to bring all personal and household effects you have owned, used or had in your possession before getting your immigrant status. You will not have to pay duty or taxes on any of these items, but customs may require receipts to prove when they were acquired. An exception could be your mattresses. To import those, you must have them cleaned and fumigated and get a certificate (to accompany the mattress) that is signed by the exporter attesting to the fact the mattresses have been cleaned and fumigated. The certificate must also give complete details of how they were cleaned and fumigated and must include a statement that the procedure was actually conducted. It may be simpler to buy new in Canada.

When you go through Canadian customs you must bring a list of goods you have with you and a list of goods you are having shipped over. The list should include the items' serial and model numbers and approximate value. The shipping list will be stamped by customs and there is no time limit for when those goods must be brought in. Business and commercial equipment is subject to duties and taxes and the amount varies widely from item to item.

To find out more, you can call your Canadian Embassy or consulate or get in touch with customs in Canada (see Useful Addresses on page 209).

Major Appliances	
Refrigerator	$900 – $10,000
Washing machine	$450 – $2,000
Tumble dryer	$400 – $1,500
Vacuum cleaner	$150 – $1,500
Oven/stove	$500 – $3,000
Houseware	
Microwave oven	$150 – $750
Toaster (two-slice)	$16 – $85
Iron	$40 – $120
Blender	$45 – $170
Food processor	$85 – $220
Toaster oven	$30 – $150
Kettle	$20 – $45
Mixer	$20 – $100
Coffee maker	$30 – $300
Bath and Bedroom	
Mattress and boxspring bed (double size)	$300 – $1,800
Towels (one bath towel)	$6 – $60
Sheets (double bed set)	$30 – $100
(single bed set)	$20 – $80
Shower curtain	$10 – $60
Pillow (regular size)	$20 – $250
Electronics	
Television (27″)	$450 – $1,000
VCR	$120 – $450
DVD	$200 – $600
Stereo mini system (CD player, radio)	$200 – $1,200
Clock radio	$15 – $200
Cordless phone	$70 – $300
Non-cordless phone	$10 – $150
Computer system	$500 – $6,000

Fig. 8. Sample household goods prices, in Canadian dollars.

⑦

Getting a Job

Choosing a career path is not an easy decision. You may wish to continue in the occupation you are in now or want to try something new. Finding the right job and working environment can make all the difference to your quality of life. If you are coming on a temporary working visa or a working holiday visa, you might be less concerned about what job you actually do because your main priority is to sample Canadian life. Even in that situation, getting a good and agreeable work placement can only make life more enjoyable.

APPLYING FOR A SOCIAL INSURANCE NUMBER

No one can legally work in Canada without a **SIN**. It is a unique number that a person is assigned that enables him or her to get a job, pay income tax and receive benefits (Employment Insurance, Social Assistance, etc.). As a newcomer you are likely to receive an application when you first arrive, but if you do not you can go to any Human Resources and Social Development Canada (HRSDC) office. Branches are listed in the phone book. To apply you need to show your birth certificate, immigration visa and passport as well as pay a small fee. You can also get applications at Canada Post Offices and at agencies that help immigrants.

Once you are hired your new employer will ask for your **Social Insurance Number**. You are not obliged to give it before then.

HAVING THE RIGHT QUALIFICATIONS

It cannot be stressed enough that before deciding to go to Canada you should ensure that your educational and training qualifications are accepted here if you want to do the job you do now. Just because Immigration Canada gives more points on the permanent resident application for certain occupations does not mean that you will be able to continue in that job once in Canada.

The reason more points are given for highly educated individuals is that the Canadian government feels those people are more inclined to work hard and succeed in whatever they do. It is a sad truth that many engineers, doctors and other professionals end up in low-paying, low-skill jobs because their degrees are not recognised in Canada. Often, an immigrant is required to undertake many years of equivalency training, at the immigrant's expense. Sometimes what is needed is Canadian experience, which means the immigrant has to undertake some volunteer work in his or her field before being hired in a paid position.

In terms of trade workers like electricians, carpenters and tool and dye makers, qualifications often do stand up as long as the immigrant has enough work experience. You will still have to pass a licensing exam, however. Make sure that you bring to Canada all your original certificates, documents and letters of recommendations.

The first step in finding out whether your credentials will be recognised in Canada is to contact the **Canadian Information Centre for International Credentials** or other credential checking services (see Useful Addresses). It's best to do this before you come to Canada, or at least make it one of the first things you do when you arrive.

The federal government recently launched the first phase of its **Foreign Credentials Referral Office (FCRO)**, which will serve as another point of contact for information for newcomers.

If your job is considered a regulated profession in Canada, you will probably have to deal with a professional association. There is a long list of regulated professions, but to give you some idea, they include doctors, engineers, lawyers, nurses and teachers. Professional associations often have internal evaluation services before granting someone a licence to work in that field, regardless of what evaluation is given by an external credential assessment service. And it can work very differently province to province. To find out what additional requirements you might have to meet, consult your specific professional association in the province where you intend to live.

Impending labour shortages, especially in terms of skilled workers, are forcing changes to the way immigrants' credentials are being evaluated and to government policy in creating opportunities for immigrants. That has included legislation (in Ontario) which forces professional associations to treat immigrants more fairly when assessing credentials and the creation of designated residency places for foreign-trained doctors. But challenges remain.

LOCATION, LOCATION, LOCATION

You might choose a city because you have family or friends there, but if you are free to go wherever you like it is wise to take stock of what different locales do and do not offer.

Unemployment rate

This varies enormously from province to province (see Figure 9). If you have a particular skill needed by a province with high unemployment, the high rate should not deter you from moving there. The overall unemployment rate in Canada is 6.1 per cent as of June 2007.

Minimum wage

Each province and territory has a general minimum wage (see Figure 10) although some have lower minimum wages for workers under 18, for people who do bartending work (and other work that usually involves tips) and for less experienced workers. Students and women make up a greater proportion of minimum wage workers, but that's not to infer that women do not hold senior positions. Minimum wage jobs are highly concentrated in the restaurant and retail industries.

Incentives

Some provincial governments offer incentives for certain types of professionals and workers in order for them to move away from urban areas to areas that need their services. Medical doctors are one example. Some provincial governments will pay doctors more to set up practices in what they call 'underserviced' areas. Some provinces are more in need of tradespeople than others are, depending on the predominant industries there. Alberta, because of its oil industry, is one of those provinces, although most provinces are experiencing some shortage of skilled tradespeople.

Province	Unemployment rate (June 2007)
Newfoundland and Labrador	13.1%
Prince Edward Island	10.5%
Nova Scotia	8.1%
New Brunswick	6.8%
Quebec	6.9%
Ontario	6.5%
Manitoba	4.6%
Saskatchewan	4.4%
Alberta	3.8%
British Columbia	4.4%

Source: Statistics Canada Labour Force Survey
Rates are seasonally adjusted

Fig. 9. Provincial uneployment figures.

Province	Minimum wage/hour
Newfoundland and Labrador	$7.70 ($8.00 on 1 April 2008)
Prince Edward Island	$7.50
Nova Scotia	$7.60 ($7.15 for inexperienced persons)
New Brunswick	$7.25
Quebec	$8.00 ($7.25 for those receiving gratuities)
Ontario	$8.00 ($7.50 for students under 18)*
Manitoba	$8.00
Saskatchewan	$7.95
Alberta	$7.00
British Columbia	$8.00**
Northwest Territories	$8.25
Yukon	$8.37
Nunavut	$8.50

* $6.95 for liquor servers.
** $6.00 for first job/entry-level until 500 hours accumulated.

Fig. 10. Provincial minimum wages.

There are many other types of occupations eligible for incentives and they change from time to time depending on demand.

Other factors

Some regions have inherent challenges or opportunities you may want to consider. For example, the economic boom in Alberta has created an amazing number of jobs, but growth is so fast and exponential, that there is now a shortage of housing and social services for all the people headed there. In Ottawa, the home of the federal government, the economy is very stable, but getting a job in that city often requires bilingualism (English and French) and getting a job with the government can involve a very lengthy security clearance process. Canadian citizens are given priority when jobs with the federal government arise.

There is sometimes more to consider than your own desires. If you are bringing over a family, you will want to find a location that suits the needs of everyone. You will want to ensure that there are job opportunities for your partner and a good school not too far away. Day care, something you may require for your children if you and your partner both work, is not always easy to find and can be very costly. Quebec subsidises day care in a major way and so it is less expensive in that province than others.

LOOKING FOR A JOB

You should start your search even before you leave your home country, even if it's just to get an idea of what's out there. For example, British newspapers sometimes carry Canadian job advertisements. You can also check relevant trade journals or order specialist publications from Canada. See Useful Addresses for the addresses to contact for such publications in addition to Internet jobsites and other useful contacts for some of the organisations mentioned below.

Human Resources and Social Development Canada's 'Service Canada' centres, specialise in helping people find jobs. The phone book will tell you where the nearest centre is to you or go to www.servicecanada.gc.ca. There are general postings on bulletin boards at the centres as well as counsellors who can help you.

Contacting an employment agency or head hunter, either in your home country or in Canada, is another starting point. Almost all Canadian newspapers are on the World Wide Web and you can try searching their classifieds. Be aware, however, that many employers who advertise in papers and through agencies are looking for immediate help.

Many jobs are not advertised at all. Hearing about a job opening through a friend of a friend of a friend is quite common. If you have any contacts already working in Canada, have them keep an ear out for you and an eye on internal postings.

Another tactic is to call companies that are in your specific field of work, even if they're not advertising. This is especially useful for the trades who are always looking for people and often don't bother advertising because if they always advertised when they needed someone, they'd have a permanent ad in the paper. For non-trades professions, most companies have specific human resources departments that can tell you if there are any openings.

It will be much easier to look for a job when you finally reach Canada. There are non-profit organisations existing solely to help newcomers find jobs.

Each province has different programmes run by different not-for-profit organisations. HRSDC offices can point you in the right direction and tell you whether you are eligible for government-sponsored skill training programmes that might help you improve your job prospects.

Once you have ideas of what posts you want to apply for, you need to send in a cover letter and résumé. Remember that companies receive hundreds of applications. It is important that yours stands out.

Writing the cover letter

If you are applying from overseas you should indicate in your cover letter when you expect to get your immigrant status or your work authorisation (see section on working visas later in this chapter and in Chapter 3) if you do not have it already.

The purpose of a cover letter is to highlight aspects of your résumé as well as information about yourself that is not in it (travel, second language, past promotions etc.). Write about specific work experience or training that is directly relevant to the job you are applying for. State why you are interested in the job and what you can bring to it and the organisation. Try to get your personality across a bit as well.

Use good quality paper and envelopes. The letter and address on the envelope should all be typewritten and make sure there are no spelling mistakes. The cover letter is the first thing a potential employer will see. In many cases if it does not stand out or if it is sloppy in any way, the person will toss it and the attached résumé in a 'no' pile right away without even looking at the résumé.

Composing the résumé

Because companies receive so many résumés, they usually do not spend a great deal of time reading them on first glance. For this reason it is best to keep your résumé to two to four pages. There are varying opinions on how best to format a Curriculum Vitae, or 'CV', but general principles do apply. If your strong suit is employment history then put that first, but if your education stands out it should go first instead. Always list the most recent experience first within your work history and education sections.

When you are applying for an assortment of positions at various companies, it does not hurt to create different résumés, each tailored to the job and/or company to which it will be sent. Figure 11 shows a fictional sample résumé. This is a very brief résumé. You may wish yours to be 'fleshier' and to describe your various positions to a greater extent. You can also put a section at the very top, called 'summary of qualifications', which should list five skills you have that are generally related to the job you are applying for. A person with more experience than Jill Doe would continue on a second page. A second page could be used to list volunteer work and other work experience or extra curricular activities if you are fresh out of university. You can also add a line listing hobbies or interests. You never know if a fellow hiking enthusiast or gardener is the one screening the résumés!

Jill Doe

14 Blackburn Road
Suffolk JW2 46X
England
jdoe@email.com
Tel: 44-1473-290-821
Fax: 44-1473-290-263

JOB OBJECTIVE: Financial services marketing manager.

MARKETING EXPERIENCE

ATK Marketing Inc.   2000 to date
Brand manager

● Responsible for marketing line of CD ROMs.

Nichemarketing Ltd   1995–1998
Marketing representative

● Promoted financial products for mutual fund client.

FINANCIAL INDUSTRY EXPERIENCE

Bowman Mutual Funds   1998–2000
Financial assistant

● Assisted broker in all aspects of financial services.

● Co-ordinated stock and asset research.

EDUCATION

Penticton School of Economics   1991–1995
BA Honours in Economics and Political Science
Dean's List 1987–1990

Lakeside Secondary   1985–1991
General Certificate of Education A Levels in Maths, Statistics,
Economics and English

OTHER SKILLS/DETAILS

● Member of the Financial Planners Association of England.

● Computer skills: word processing, spreadsheets and graphics.

References available on request

Fig. 11. Sample résumé.

Explaining gaps

If your résumé contains gaps in employment or education, it is important to explain them in your cover letter. Do so honestly and as positively as possible. Were you actively looking for a job? Undergoing further training? Or maybe you were travelling abroad? In terms of education, if you did not complete your studies, point out what you did achieve (e.g. finished two years of radio and telecommunications studies). If you do not explain holes in your résumé, the person hiring will imagine worse reasons than what really happened.

Nowadays, changing jobs or careers is often looked upon as a positive thing. Employers like to know you have a range of skills. However, if you were at a different job every few months, that would be a problem. If there's a logical reason for you moving about a lot, give it. But if you just did not like the jobs or the employers, steer clear of saying so. Highlight any long-term commitments you did make during that time such as taking part-time studies in the evenings over the course of a few years.

Supplying references

You do not need to supply references until asked. Have ready a list of three referees, ones who you know will speak well of you, to fax or send to the company when it requests them. If they ask if they can call your previous employers and there is one you would rather they not call, weigh the options. If that employer will simply be less than enthusiastic about you, it may not be worth sounding the alarms. But if you know that they will speak badly of you, tell the company that you would prefer that it not call that particular reference. You will probably have to explain why, so be honest but positive. Do not say how much you hate the person or they hate you. Maybe allude to creative differences or that you got along but they were unhappy with you because you left.

Assets

Canadian employers value some assets above all others and it is useful to know what those are:

◆ Strong grasp of both spoken and written **English.**

◆ Ability in **more than one language**. For many government jobs French is a must, but any second language is a plus.

◆ **Experience**. If you have ever worked in Canada before, even if only on a working holiday or temporary work visa, that will be a definite asset.

◆ **Training**. Canada seeks workers with high credentials. Employers like people with a higher education or people with a great deal of practical training.

◆ **Computer skills**. There is a special initiative now to entice computer specialists to come and work in Canada. See Chapter 3 for more details.

◆ **Driver's licence**. As soon as you can when you arrive, start the process of obtaining one from the province in which you're residing (see Chapter 9).

The interview

There are so many interview tips floating about that it is difficult to know where to start. First, research the company. Nothing looks worse than not knowing about your potential employer in the interview. Many factors play into giving a good interview and even if you do everything right, you may still not land the job. But knowing right from wrong is half the battle.

Appearance

Be clean and tidy. This includes your hair, nails and clothes. Men should shave or tidy their beard. Women should not wear a lot of makeup and although it is advisable for both sexes to dress conservatively (a suit) and modestly, it cannot hurt to have some style. In other words, do not go so far that you look dowdy.

Attitude

Be positive and enthusiastic. Be early, never late. Sit a bit forward in the chair; it looks as if you are disinterested if you lean back. In all your nervousness, try not to forget to smile. When you shake the interviewer's hand, make it a firm handshake, even if you are female. In Canada it is not thought unladylike to provide a firm handshake. A limp one conveys weakness.

Answering questions

Be concise but thorough. Avoid both monosyllabic answers or ones that ramble on. If you feel the question is too general or you do not understand it, do not forge ahead aimlessly. Ask for clarification.

Catching you offguard

Interviewers undertake many methods to get at who you are. Some tactics are fairly unorthodox (like suddenly leaving the room and then coming back in). Be prepared and no matter what, stay calm. It is imperative that you sit down a night or two before, come up with a list of potential questions and then practise your answers. But, do not go into the interview with a script in your head, flexibility is key.

At the end

As the interview winds down it usually comes to an end with the interviewer asking if you have anything else to add. Never decline this offer. Perhaps you forgot a point in a previous answer that you think is important. Perhaps a question was never asked that would have addressed something you would like to be known about yourself. However, if the interviewer does not offer this opportunity, do not rush in at the end with additional information, unless it is really important. Instead, ask a question or two about the job or when you will next hear from the company, but don't enquire about salary at this time. If the interviewer actually asks if you have any questions, again never decline. Always have one or two ready otherwise you will look disinterested. Do not forget to say thank you.

After
Send a thank you note to the interviewer or interviewers if there was more than one. Be simple and to the point, but do not delay.

If you have not heard back about the job within the time frame they indicated, call them. If you still do not hear back, call again. There's a fine line between being persistent and being too aggressive, but do not just sit and wait for the phone to ring.

If you didn't get the job, ask politely for feedback about what you could improve upon in terms of credentials or interview performance for the future.

If you're finding the job search isn't going well, some cities have not-for-profit skill development programmes that include practice firms. Those are places where you work for six or more weeks to brush up on both work and office social skills as well as to get advice on improving your résumé and interviewing skills. You can find out more about practice firms at HRSDC offices.

At the end of the Useful Addresses section of this book, there is a list of websites, many of which are job search and employment sites and some are specifically geared to immigrants.

DOING IT YOURSELF

Perhaps you want to start your own business or continue the one you ran in your home country. The laws and regulations pertaining to businesses in Canada are complex and vary from province to province, city to city and business to business. This chapter will simply point out a few general factors to consider.

Most of the recent economic and job growth in Canada has been due to small- and mid-size businesses. Therefore many banks are flogging small-business loans and if you have a good idea, and can sell the idea to the bank, you will get some sort of start-up money. Canadians consistently vote entrepreneurs as one of the most respected professions in Canada; but running your own business means long hours and a great deal more financial risk than if you work for someone else.

Taxes in Canada are quite high and some businesses just cannot survive because of them, and the Canadian market may not respond well to your product. Do not think that just because it was a success in your country it will be so in Canada. Research the Canadian market first.

At the same time, many immigrants have found that Canada's growing multicultural society has offered business opportunities, whether it's opening an ethnic food shop or other service geared to their ethnic community.

Buying a franchise

If you do not want to forge ahead with your own idea or product but still want to be your own boss, there is the option of buying a franchise business. These are often chain stores such as cafés and snack stores of which there are several in a city. You gain the security of a product that has already proved it can sell, but lose some of the autonomy of it being entirely your own business.

Also, because you are purchasing a brand that is already established, these businesses can be quite expensive to buy. But if you have the capital to put up, and you get a good location, franchises can pay off in the long run.

LOOKING AT CUSTOM AND PRACTICE

Unions

Unions are groups of working people who are organised to protect their rights in the workplace. What began as a struggle to be heard has evolved into a powerful movement. In the 19th century the first unions were formed to protect members against financial disaster in times of illness or unemployment. From the start, employers and management vehemently opposed unions.

Today nearly 4.5 million full-time paid workers belong to a union. In 2005, 429,000 workers were involved in 261 work stoppages (strikes or lockouts) that resulted in an estimated 4.1 million work days lost, a huge increase over previous years. However, that was because of the large size of the unions involved in disputes that year. In 2006, work days lost totalled more than 800,000, a record low, although the number of work stoppages was in the same range as before. Compare that with the US, where in 2006 there were only 20 strikes or lockouts, and the UK where there were 145 from September 2005 to September 2006.

Different unions exist for a variety of work. **Craft unions** join together skilled workers in a particular craft or trade. **Industrial unions** are for all workers in a single industry, whatever the skill. Some unions have mandatory membership while others are optional. Union fees are usually deducted from the pay cheque.

Unions are organised into locals that represent union members in a specific workplace or local area. Various unions are grouped together under Labour Councils and each province has a provincial Federation of Labour. Nationally, most unions belong to the Canadian Labour Congress, while others belong to the Canadian Federation of Labour (the building trades unions), the Confederation of Canadian Unions (small group of nationalist unions) and the Confédération des Syndicats Nationaux.

Holidays
It is often a great shock to Europeans when they come to Canada and find out those many weeks of holidays they used to enjoy are no longer. Canada just does not offer such luxuries!

Most full-time permanent jobs offer two weeks off per year to start with, once you've been with the company for a certain period of time – usually six months to a year. As you continue to work at the company, that time is increased so that after three or four years you may get up to four weeks. Except for high-end jobs and professionals who work for themselves (e.g. doctors), it does not go much higher than that. Of course, there is the odd statutory day off or bank holiday, but that hardly totals much more than an additional week. Teachers get the summer off, but they often teach summer school or take professional development courses. Compared with other countries, Canada is in the middle of the pack for the average amount of hours people work.

An increasing trend is for companies to hire contract workers. Some Canadians resent this, as they desire more permanency and security, but others enjoy the flexibility of signing on for a project for a few months and then having some time off before bidding for another project.

Discrimination and harassment

Canadian laws protect people from discrimination when seeking employment and once employed. Women still, on average, earn less for equal work than men do. Sexual harassment is strictly forbidden. If you feel that you have been discriminated against or that you are being harassed, contact the Human Rights Commission in your province. If you feel you are being exploited at work, contact Human Resources and Social Development Canada or the Ministry of Labour in your province.

FOREIGN WORKERS

This category pertains to those people who are seeking to come to Canada on a temporary work visa or a working holiday visa. For more detailed information see Chapter 3.

Temporary work visa

It is not an easy process to get a temporary work visa. In most cases you need what's called a labour market opinion or confirmation from Human Resources and Social Development

Canada (HRSDC), which essentially requires that you already
have a job offer and that it meets certain requirements. If you
have a job offer from a Canadian employer, there are steps that
the employer must take in order that your work authorisation is
approved.

♦ The employer must give details of the job offer to Human
  Resources and Social Development Canada (HRSDC).

♦ An HRSDC counsellor will verify that the offer meets wage and
  working condition standards for that occupation. An employer
  cannot offer you or pay you less than the going rate.

♦ The counsellor will consider several factors when deciding on the
  opinion. He or she will look at whether the work will lead to
  further job creation/retention for Canadians, if the work will
  mean skills and knowledge will be passed on to the benefit of
  Canadians and if the work is likely to fill a labour shortage. The
  counsellor will also look at whether your employment will
  negatively affect the settlement of a labour dispute.

♦ Finally, what might be the stickiest point is whether the
  employer has made reasonable effort to find or train a Canadian
  for the job. And in many cases there is a Canadian who *can* do
  the job. One way to combat this is for the employer to prove
  your set of skills is unique or so superior that no ordinary
  Canadian would do. However, it's questionable whether an
  employer would go to such lengths to hire you if there are
  Canadians willing and able.

The above steps are somewhat different than they used to be, as
the immigration and visa laws have just been changed. The old
policy of 'Canadians first' has been put aside in favour of aiming

for a 'net benefit to Canada.' But as you can see from the last
step, it's still the goal that foreign workers aren't brought in to
the detriment of Canadian workers. So, it remains to be seen how
the new laws will actually affect those wanting to come to Canada
to work.

Once the HRSDC approves the job offer, potential employees can
then apply for a work permit from their local Canadian Embassy,
High Commission or Consulate in their country.

Some jobs are automatically exempt from HRSDC approval and it
is a good idea to check with an HRSDC office or with a Canadian
embassy or consulate first before going through all the trouble for
nothing. There will be a processing fee.

To get your permit, you will have to establish that you meet the
criteria of the job and provide documentation such as educational
certificates, employment references and work samples. You also
will probably have to get a medical examination at your own
expense to assure the Canadian government that you are healthy
before entering the country.

If all goes well you will get your permit and be on your way. The
permit outlines that you can work at a specific job, for a specific
employer and for a specific time.

When you arrive, bring your permit, your passport and any other
travel documents you need. It is the employer's responsibility to
arrange for your medical cover when you arrive, but make sure it
is arranged before you arrive.

If while you are in Canada you discover that your work will take longer or your job changes, you will have to apply to change your permit 30 days in advance of its expiry date.

Residents of the US, Greenland or Saint Pierre and Miquelon can apply for a work permit at a port of entry to Canada, but these special people must still have confirmation of an offer of employment.

Working holiday programmes

Working holiday visas usually involve age restrictions. Some are for university students only while others are employer-specific and work more like a temporary work visa. Canada has different agreements with different countries, which cannot possibly all be listed here. In general, such visas are restricted to 18–30-year-olds. Quebec has its own agreements with particular countries, especially Belgium and France.

In some cases a medical examination will be required before a visa will be issued.

Australia

Canada's agreement with Australia is, perhaps, its most open one, mainly because the programme is not restricted to students. In 2007 Canada had a quota of 7,750 working holiday visas for Australians and at the beginning of August a little more than 2,700 remained. Australians, aged 18–30 (inclusive), are eligible. The visa is a one-year, non-renewable, open permit visa. That means you don't have to find an employer before going to Canada in order to get the visa, but you can get such a visa only once in your life. Australians on this permit look for work once they arrive. Other criteria include, but are not limited to, proof of having enough funds to sustain yourself (AUD $4,000) and not having a criminal record and passing a medical examination. You should also have a valid Australian passport that will not expire during the year away. In 2007 the fee was AUD $165.

Australians can download the application form from www.whpcanada.org.au or order it from the Canadian Consulate General in Sydney. However the application form must be sent in by post and not sent in by email or dropped off in person.

New Zealand
A similar programme to the Australian one is available for citizens of New Zealand. The quota for 2007 was 2,000 and at the beginning of August there were 600 places left. The fee is NZ$200. There is a link on the Australian WHP website for the New Zealand programme (NZWHP) or go to: http://www.dfait-maeci.gc.ca/asia/whp/intro-en.asp

Student work abroad schemes
This is how most young people from other countries get to have a working holiday in Canada. Unlike the Australian programme, these programmes require that foreigners are either full-time university students, or have recently graduated.

The Student Work Abroad Program (SWAP)
The programme is offered to people from the UK, Ireland, Australia, New Zealand and the USA as well as a number of other countries including Argentina, India, Poland, Slovakia, South Africa, France and Germany. Go to www.swap.ca for the complete list of participating countries.

Generally it provides a one-year, non-renewable open-permit visa, except to Americans, for whom it's a six-month visa. Age limits vary from country to country, so it's best to check for your own, but generally it's for 18 to 30 year olds. The programme doesn't find travellers work, but its registration fee does ensure the necessary working visa, two nights' accommodation upon arrival and various other services.

For more information, contact a student travel agency in your country or a Travel Cuts agency in Canada. Your university campus placement and career centre may have information as well.

British Universities North American Club (BUNAC)

Under this programme, one-year, non-renewable working holiday visas are available to students from the UK who are taking a year off from university or who have just finished their 'A' levels and hold an unconditional offer to attend university. You must be between 18 and 35 years old. Applicants must show proof they are returning to school or continuing with higher education. BUNAC also has a programme for non-students. Enquire at the Canadian High Commission in London or go to www.bunac.org.uk BUNAC's website.

A similar programme exists for Irish citizens through USIT. (www.usitnow.ie). For students in Finland go to www.cimo.fi. Swedish students should apply through the International Employment Office (in Sweden phone: 46 23 93700). None exists for students in Denmark, Norway, Iceland or Greenland.

British students can also take part in a volunteer programme during their 'gap year'. Go to www.direct.gov.uk/en/youngpeople for more information.

Council on International Educational Exchange (CIEE)
Council Exchanges work like those already listed above. France, Germany and the US have programmes with Canada.
Requirements vary for each country, but generally applicants have to be a full-time student or recent graduate and be under the age of 31. Americans get a five-month work visa. For more information see www.ciee.org.uk

Other schemes
Argentina, Austria, Costa Rica, Czech Republic, Italy, Ghana, Mexico, the Netherlands, Peru, Poland, Portugal, Slovakia, Spain and South Africa all have some sort of agreement with Canada for students wanting to work abroad. Check with the Canadian Visa Post for your country or with a local student travel agency.

Live-in Caregiver Program
Caregivers are people who are qualified to care independently for children, elderly or the disabled. There are some requirements you have to meet in order to participate in this programme.

◆ You must have the equivalent of a Canadian high school education.

◆ You need to have six months of full-time training or 12 months of full-time paid working experience in the field or occupation that is related to the live-in caregiver job you are looking for. The paid work experience must include six months of continuous employment with one employer. Examples of relevant fields are early childhood education, geriatric care, paediatric nursing and first aid. Your experience must have been gained within the three years prior to your application.

♦ You must be able to speak, read and understand either English or French.

The work permit is usually for one year and must be renewed for the next year before it expires. To renew it the employer must provide a signed contract showing the job as a live-in caregiver is being offered for another year. However, now the Canadian government is issuing permits valid for up to three years and three months.

As a live-in caregiver you will live in your employers' home. If for any reason you wish to change employers, you may do so. You cannot be deported for quitting your job, but you must find a new employer, and you must have applied for and received a new work permit before working for the new employer because the work visa for this programme is employer specific. It's also important to note that you can change jobs only if it is to do another caregiver job. There have been some problems in the past with this programme where employers have told their caregivers they can get a supplementary job doing something else to make more money. This is not true and you can be deported if found to be working as something other than a caregiver, whether in addition to being a caregiver or instead of being a caregiver altogether. There are other conditions and regulations pertaining to this programme. To get more detailed information, contact your nearest Canadian Embassy or consulate. After completing at least two years of employment as a live-in caregiver, you can apply for permanent residence in Canada.

Other programmes

From time to time the government creates working or exchange schemes to address a particular need in the Canadian labour force or a social need. Check with your Canadian Embassy or consulate to see what is currently being offered.

8

Going to School

The education system in Canada varies from province to province because it is not a federal responsibility. But generalities do exist. First, it should be noted that 'public schools' in Canada do not mean the same thing as they do, for example, in the UK. Public schools are those funded by taxes and available free to every child. Private schools are those paid for by the parents of the child. Ninety-five per cent of all children in Canada attend public schools, which are co-educational. Teachers in all provinces must be qualified and licensed.

Generally, the school year runs from September (the day after Labour Day) to the end of June for elementary and secondary schools and from early September to the end of April for universities. There are some exceptions, however. Some public schools in Canada have been experimenting with all-year schooling with shorter holidays spread out during the year and some university programmes, especially some professional courses, run through the summer.

FUNDING/JURISDICTION

Although education is under the jurisdiction of the provinces, funding comes from all levels of government: municipal property taxes, provincial taxes and federal taxes (a portion given to the provinces through transfer payments). The federal government provides funding for post-secondary education and is responsible for the education of aboriginals, armed forces personnel and inmates of federal penal institutions.

Responsibility for the administration of elementary and secondary schools is delegated to local elected school boards or commissions. In some provinces the provincial governments have become more involved but these boards generally set local budgets, hire and negotiate with teachers (who are unionised) and shape school curriculum within provincial guidelines.

It is usually the individual schools that set, conduct and mark their examinations but some provinces are heading back to province-wide exams, much to the chagrin of some students!

In recent years, there has been much conflict between the provincial governments and school boards, especially in Ontario. The issues are complex and it is not possible go into detail here. But basically public school boards say they are underfunded and can't deliver the education they should with the money they're given. The province has put more money into the system, but not as much as was asked for. Part of the problem is while the province holds the purse strings, the board still has the responsibility to negotiate contracts with teachers and staff. The result has been budget deficits and cuts to special education programmes, as well as school closures (the students are merged with another school).

OUTLINING LEVELS OF INSTRUCTION

This really depends on the individual province, but generally primary education starts at the kindergarten level (junior and senior) at the age of 4 or 5 and continues to the end of grade 6, although some schools continue to grade 8. In some provinces there is a junior high level, either grades 7 and 8 or 7, 8 and 9. Secondary education, or high school, goes from grade 9 or 10 to grade 11 or 12, again depending on the province.

Pre-school

Some parents choose to place their children in a school-like setting before it is legally required to do so. For pre-school, children are usually aged 3 and 4 and attend only a half-day of 'class'. It is not a structured setting and the focus is on the basics: the alphabet, numbers, arts and crafts, songs and play. Studies have shown that children's minds are very absorbent in their first five years of life. Pre-school can enhance a child's vocabulary, motor skills and social skills and is a good option as an alternative to regular day-care if parents work.

Kindergarten to grade 6

Junior kindergarten is usually just half a day, but after that children attend for a full day, although for the younger grades a rest time is usually ensured. In elementary school, children have the same teacher for all their subjects with a few exceptions. Special education and French classes are taught by teachers trained particularly for those courses. The curriculum emphasises the basic subjects of reading, writing, maths, geography, history, science, social studies and introductory arts. Small tests and projects are assigned as well as homework. These school years often involve special projects, field trips and dramatic presentations (Christmas pageants, musical recitals, etc.). In some provinces children get the opportunity to learn a musical instrument like the recorder or even play in a small school band in grades 5 and 6. In some provinces enriched or accelerated programmes are available for academically gifted students, as are special programmes for slower learners and students with disabilities.

Grades 7 and 8

For the purposes of this book, it will be assumed that these two grades are attended at a separate school and are not grouped with grade 9. For those schools that go from grade 6 to 8 or for those schools that include grade 9, the curriculum is not any different. The only difference is how the levels are divided.

A child in grade 7 is about 12 or 13 years of age. At this stage a lot more is expected from the students and subjects are studied in greater detail and depth. Often, each subject has a separate teacher so that students have a 'homeroom' teacher who teaches one subject and then they travel together as a class to other teachers to get instruction in the other subjects. Students do not choose their subjects; the courses are all mandatory. They are instructed in English, French (not all provinces), maths, science, history, geography and physical education. In many schools, mid-year and end-of-year examinations are given in addition to tests, assignments and essays. Enrichment and remedial learning programmes are available as well.

High school

By law, children must attend school from the age of 6 until the age of 15 or 16, depending on the province. Ontario recently brought in legislation making attendance in school mandatory until 18 or graduation, whichever happens first. The new law includes fines for parents who allow their children to drop out before that time, and fines for employers who hire students during school hours when the students should be in school. Also, students who have dropped out of school before they're 18 can have their driver's licence suspended; or cannot obtain a driver's licence if they don't already have one. Most provinces have grades 9 to 12, but Quebec students finish in grade 11 before going into the CEGEP system (more on that later). Ontario recently eliminated grade 13 to be in line with the rest of the provinces (other than Quebec). The last students to go through the five-year system graduated in 2003.

High school entails taking compulsory courses and having the option of choosing electives. Some schools offer different levels of courses and both academic-oriented and trade-oriented courses, while others are only academic and offer only the highest difficulty level of academic courses.

All schools have certain credits, which you must take if you want to pursue university or college. These are usually the courses required in the last year of high school. Most universities look at the mean average grade of these courses when assessing a student's application. In Quebec, after grade 11, students go to a CEGEP, which is like a junior college, before heading to university.

If students have advanced skills in a subject, beyond the grade to which they are automatically designated because of their age, they can be tested and put ahead a year (or more) so that they remain challenged. This does not mean they automatically obtain credits for the courses they skipped, but it does mean they have more room in their timetable for other courses.

At some high schools there is also the option of enrolling in enriched courses that provide advanced-level academia for students who have shown exceptional ability in a particular subject like English or maths. There are also special programmes for students with learning challenges, such as attention deficit disorder, autism, dyslexia, etc. In some schools those students are integrated into the regular classroom with help from additional education assistants and therapists (occupational, speech, etc.) while in other schools, there are separate classes for those students.

CATEGORISING TYPES OF SCHOOLS

Deciding what school to enrol your children in is a personal choice. There is no right or wrong answer to the question of what kind of school is better. There are pros and cons for all the choices and, of course, it comes down to what's convenient for where you live and what you are able to afford.

Public schools

Most students go to public schools. They may be less elite and specialised than private schools but parents who advocate public schools say that they offer just as good a level of education as private schools as long as the student works hard. There is often a broader selection of courses and the same amount of extracurricular activities as at private schools, but in some provinces public schools face funding problems that have resulted in large classes and the downsizing of special programmes. Public schools are co-ed, books do not cost extra and neither do most field trips. Sometimes extra fees are charged for special trips. But schools often undertake fundraising drives to raise money for such trips or projects. Public schools are non-denominational and any religious instruction is usually given in the context of a world religions course.

Private schools

Smaller classes, a focus on academic courses and superior athletic facilities are what private schools offer in comparison to the public school system, but it comes at a price. Not including extras like the cost of uniforms, athletic equipment and books, the yearly price tag ranges from about $10,000 to $20,000 per child. Yet parents of children who go to private school still pay taxes that fund a public system they don't use. Because of that, five Canadian provinces (B.C., Alberta, Saskatchewan, Manitoba and Quebec) give some funding directly to some independent schools.

Of course, most private schools offer scholarships and bursaries. To get in, prospective students must pass an entrance exam in most cases.

Private schools offer longer vacations for students under the premise that the time students do spend in class is more rigorous and demanding than time spent in public schools. Most of the private schools are girls-only or boys-only but there are a few that have become co-ed in the face of financial difficulty. Also included in this category are schools such as those offering the Montessori educational method. Boarding is available at many private schools for families that want to send their children to a private school quite a distance from their home. Additional fees for this are, of course, applicable, sometimes upwards of $7,000 a year.

Separate schools/alternative schools

Provincial legislation allows for the establishment of separate schools by religious groups. Mostly Roman Catholic, these schools offer a curriculum based on religion, from kindergarten through to secondary level. There are schools of other religious denomination as well. Uniforms are usually required and some schools are segregated by gender while others are mixed.

Both Alberta and Ontario fund Catholic schools as they do public schools. Children do not have to be Catholic to attend. Alberta also funds some Protestant and charter schools on the same basis as they do public schools. (Charter schools are independent schools that have performance-based charters, or contracts, with the province.)

Schools of other denominations are not publicly funded and parents interested in having their children educated separately must pay for it themselves. This has been a source of great controversy.

Alternative schools are those that provide an 'opening learning' environment for students, where they can work at their own pace.

French immersion

There are both French and English language schools throughout Canada, with French schools being most numerous in Quebec. Outside Quebec, French public schools are often referred to as schools with French immersion programmes in which all subjects are taught in French. These schools begin in the early grades, as it is considerably easier for children to learn a new language from an early age. If you want your children to go to one of these schools at a later stage, they will have to be tested to see where their language skills stand.

EXAMINING FACILITIES

Most elementary schools have an indoor gymnasium and an outdoor playground. Secondary school facilities depend on the size of the school, with some having more than one gymnasium and most having a regulation-sized sports field for outdoor sports. Outdoor tracks and swimming pools are common for secondary schools and some even have weight rooms. Due to tight funding the upkeep of such facilities has been a struggle. Private schools in the cities have less expansive grounds than those in the suburbs or those outside the city altogether, but many private schools have extensive playing grounds, even if housed downtown.

ENROLLING

The first step is to arrange a visit with the school. For public school there are restrictions in terms of choice. Normally you need to send your child to the school in your district. By calling your school board you can find out which school that is. If the local school doesn't have a special programme your child may be allowed to go to another school further away that does have it. To enrol you need to bring your child's:

◆ birth or baptismal certificate
◆ immigration landing papers
◆ passport
◆ medical records (vaccination certificate)
◆ any previous school records.

The school will decide which grade your child should attend and if they need special lessons in English or French. Many schools offer English or French as second language (ESL or FSL) classes to help students catch up. If you think your children may have been incorrectly placed, talk to their teacher, guidance counsellor or school principal.

If you wish to acquire general information about Canadian schools before arriving in Canada, you may contact the **Canadian School Boards Association** (CSBA) (see Useful Addresses).

SCHOOL BREAKS

In elementary and high schools, students get two months off in the summer (July and August), approximately two weeks at Christmas time and a week in March (called March or Spring Break). Private schools often get longer periods of time off, with a couple of extra weeks in June and an extra week for March Break. People of religions other than Christianity are entitled to take off their holy days as well, such as Ramadan and Rosh Hashanah, although students have to catch up on the work they missed on those days.

In university, students get approximately four months off, from May to the end of August as well as a week in February. This is based on a regular eight-month programme. Students at semestered universities and those in co-op programmes might have school or a work placement in the summer months.

GOING ON TO HIGHER EDUCATION

Every year about 180,000 university degrees and 600,000 college diplomas are granted in Canada. For most Canadians getting a university or college education has become an important step in getting a good job. Canada spends (public and private funds) 5.2 per cent of its GDP on education. Investment in education, as a percentage of the country's GDP has declined over the years, but Canada is still ahead of the US (5.1%) and the United Kingdom (4.8%). In terms of attainment of post-secondary education, Canada has one of the highest levels of any country in the Organisation for Economic Co-Operation and Development (OECD). Forty-five per cent of 25- to 64-year-olds hold what's known as a tertiary degree.

Although students straight out of high school make up the majority at post-secondary institutions, the number of mature students is on the rise.

Universities

Canadian universities have been through some turbulent times of late due to huge cuts in funding coupled with increased enrolment, but tuition is still relatively low in contrast to comparable US schools. Every possible programme is offered somewhere, but most schools fall under specific categories such as medical/ doctoral, primarily undergraduate or liberal arts only. Therefore not every programme is offered at all of Canada's 40-plus universities. Most have extensive full-time, part-time and continuing education programmes. As mentioned previously, the academic year lasts from September to mid-May although some programmes run through the summer. Some courses are also offered in the summer if you choose to accelerate your studies or if you unfortunately fail a course.

A general undergraduate degree, if done full-time, usually takes three years, while an honours degree takes four years and often involves doing a thesis or major research project. Masters programmes vary from one to three years and PhD programmes range from four to seven years. Professional degrees like medicine or law usually require an undergraduate degree while other professional degrees like engineering (PEng) or a Masters of Business (MBA) require a couple of years of working in the relevant field either before or after the degree programme. Basically, graduate studies are more research-based, the admission materials required are more extensive and tuition often much higher.

The study period for a law degree (LL.B) lasts three years after which the student articles with a law firm for one year before taking the bar examinations to become a licensed lawyer. There are graduate degrees in law as well. Lawyers who move to another province must pass the bar exam for that province. Degrees in medicine (MD) take three to four years, then a student interns for one to two years after which they are licensed by the provincial medical boards. However, for speciality medicine (heart surgeons, neurologists, etc.) internships are far longer. Students are paid while interning.

Programmes such as business, engineering and architecture are offered at some universities as a co-op degree, which means part of your study includes working during your course in your relevant field. You study for two or three terms (a few months each) and then work for a term, then study for another couple of terms and work another term. The degree takes longer to obtain (e.g. architecture can take seven years) but in turn you get practical experience, make money to help fund your studies and hopefully get your foot in the door somewhere. Universities try to help students to find their work placements.

Universities range in size from a total enrolment of 800 to 60,000. Some are in a city's downtown while others are in more suburban or rural settings.

Applying
Canadian citizens and landed immigrants essentially go through the same process when applying to Canadian universities. There are application forms and varying fees for each university you apply for. For Ontario universities, because there are so many and because Ontario has the largest population, the limit on how many any one student can apply to is three. In applying to Ontario universities, students must go through a central application centre, the Ontario Universities Application Centre (OUAC) in Guelph, Ontario. OUAC requires students to rank their top three choices of school and programme and to pay one overall fee. For part-time studies, students need to apply directly to the universities.

Tuition
Full-time tuition varies greatly from school to school so it is

difficult to put a general figure on it. Suffice to say it's far from free. For a liberal arts programme, undergraduate science degree or business degree a student could be looking at tuition from $2,000 to $14,000 per year. For the 2006–2007 academic year, the average tuition for one year of an undergraduate programme in Canada was $4,347. Since 1990 tuition fees have increased, on average, seven per cent per year. Some professional programmes have been deregulated so that the universities are no longer subject to government tuition caps, meaning tuition for such programmes is much higher. The federal government, through its **Canada Student Loans Program**, assists students who can prove that they do not have sufficient resources to fund their own studies. The provinces have complementary loan programmes but even with both a federal and provincial loan, most students will have to work part-time and in the summer to meet the costs of school and living. However, the way some of the provincial loan programmes are set up, the more you work the less loan money you get. Most loan payments are due in monthly instalments plus interest after six months from graduating, although during that six-month grace period, interest is accruing. However the annual interest you pay on your loans is tax deductible. Also, some loan programmes have a loan forgiveness option in extreme circumstances.

Universities and even some corporations offer scholarships and bursaries based on academic proficiency and/or financial need. Usually a portion of tuition fees, sometimes as much as 60 per cent, is due before you start classes.

Tuition fees for foreign students are higher than for Canadians or permanent residents. See the foreign student section later in the chapter.

Books/supplies

This is where the costs can add up. Depending on the programme, your books can cost upwards of $800 for the year, sometimes much higher. Science students can also assume higher costs due to the need for lab supplies. Calculators, pens, pencils, binders, paper and white-out are the least of your concerns. Although universities have computer labs, they are often packed full and closed at night when you would most likely be doing that last-minute essay. It is usually best to get your own computer equipment, which can cost from $700 upwards depending on what you choose and need.

University life

Life at university is often about more than studying. Self-discovery, meeting people from varied backgrounds and extracurricular involvement are all part of university life. Student journalism, student government, recreational and competitive athletics, debating, Amnesty International and many other organisations are available for students to join. Many universities have clubs or organisations that are specifically geared to a common cultural or ethnic group. There is likely to be an international students office and adviser as well.

University residence/housing

Unless you are going to a university in the city in which you live already, you will probably live in a university residence or in off-campus housing. Even students who could live at home sometimes choose to move out at this time in order to be more independent, but of course doing so is more expensive. The first year of an undergraduate programme is when most students live in residence. Residences come in many shapes and sizes: small, large, new, old, co-ed (floors, not rooms) and single-sex. Some universities have limited residence space and getting a residence room is based on age (preference given to younger students), where the student comes from (local students get less preference) and grades (the higher the better). International students on visas usually have little trouble getting a residence and many large universities have international student housing. Residence rooms are usually single or double with a series of rooms, or entire halls, sharing a bathroom that usually has several sinks and showers. Some residences are in old rambling houses that provide a cosier atmosphere; some are apartment-style where there is no cafeteria and students cook for themselves. There are also residences for mature and married students.

Choosing residence

In terms of economics, residence can either be a good choice or an expensive choice, depending on the city. The price of residence often includes a meal plan and if you prefer to cook, eat out or if you simply do not eat very much, this can be expensive. In a big city where housing can be expensive residence is often a good choice, but in some cities off-campus housing is very cheap and plentiful. It's also important to point out that in many cases, the cost of residence is up front, at the beginning of the academic year, unlike the monthly rent of off-campus housing. Many students forego the economics and, in the first year, choose to live in residence for the social aspect and convenience factors. However, such residences are not only filled with first year students, 'freshmen', but also senior students. Some of these senior students take on a resident advisory role.

Residences naturally have more rules than housing in which you live independently. Quiet hours, drinking rules and who you can bring in as a guest are par for the course. Living off-campus clearly offers more independence, but one perk of residence life, aside from an easy avenue of meeting people, is that you are paying for eight months only. Off-campus housing often entails finding someone to rent your place for the summer, moving out entirely and finding a new place in September or just paying rent for four months that you're not there if you go home for the summer.

It is very difficult to estimate residence costs because they vary so greatly from city to city. You could be looking at anything from $3,500 to $6,500 (including meal plans) per year. That is in addition to tuition, books and supplies.

Choosing off-campus housing

Off-campus housing is usually shared accommodation in which a few students share a house or an apartment. Universities have housing departments to help students find both residence and off-campus accommodation. In university towns, (towns in which the university is a major fixture) housing is often cheap and student-oriented, but in big cities you are competing with all the other wannabe-renters. For example, what you find for $500 a month in Halifax, you would pay $900 or more a month for in Toronto. Leases are usually for a year but in student-oriented housing subletting (when you rent to someone else if you go home for the summer) is allowed. (See Chapter 6 for more details on how to find rental accommodation.) The chart in Figure 12 may help estimate a year's cost. It does not include medical expenses or plans, the latter being much costlier for foreign students, nor does it include clothing or other optional items. Since entertainment is such an integral part of university life, it is included.

	Non-residence	Residence
Tuition	$1,900–$14,000	$1,900–$14,000
Housing*	$2,800–$8,000	$3,500–$11,000
Books/supplies	$600–$1,600	$600–$1,600
Food	$1,600–$2,500	$600**
Transport***	$800	$600
Entertainment	$600–$1,000	$600–$1,000
TOTAL****	**$8,100-$27,900**	**$7,600-$28,300**

*Based on eight months. Costs are much less if student lives at home with parents.

**There are always food costs in addition to meal plan coverage.

***Based on public transportation including going to and from school and travelling within the city. Does not include trips home.

****These are estimates, a year at university can cost less or more depending on individual needs.

Fig. 12. Estimating a year's university costs.

Remember, however, that part of your tuition and rental expenses can be used as deductions from your income tax.

University requirements

To go to a university you must have a high school diploma or equivalent, although many universities allow adults over 25 or 30 to enter as mature students, based on their individual abilities and background rather than on previous education.

Although some schools advertise entrance cut-off grades at 65 per cent (for a liberal arts programme, sciences and other programmes are advertised as having much higher cut-offs), it is actually much more competitive than that. In other words, if you apply with a 65 per cent, you're likely not going to get in. Most schools publish an official 70 or 75 per cent cut-off and even then, you really need higher marks than that to get in.

To enter in a September class you should apply by the previous autumn, but some schools do allow January or May starts because they run on a semester basis. Regardless, apply to university a year in advance from when you want to start.

If your first language is not English, or you come from a non-English speaking country, you will probably be required to take the American Test of English as a Foreign Language (TOEFL) or another language test of the university's choice. Generally, French universities determine the level of French skills on an individual basis, which could include both written and oral tests.

Transfers and exchanges

If you have been attending another university in your own country you may be able to have some, or all, of your credits transferred to count towards your degree, but many universities do not recognise foreign credits and it is possible that you will have to start from scratch. Check with the individual university when you are applying.

If you are coming on a formal exchange you are probably in Canada for only a year or so and plan to finish your degree at the university you started at in your home country. In this case it is likely that the exchange programme ensures credit transferability, but it is always best to check first that the credits you earn in Canada will be accepted when you return home.

Passing the course

In terms of passing courses at Canadian universities, again standards vary. Some courses require you to simply earn a grade of 50 per cent or more while others can only be passed with 60 per cent or higher. Even if you pass all the courses, you may still be in trouble if you have not obtained a high enough overall average; but universities also understand about the demands of the first year as well as specific personal problems you may run into in any year. If something happens in your life that is affecting your academic work, it is best to see a counsellor in your university's academic office, or a professor or dean who you feel comfortable talking with.

To be able to get into a master's, doctoral or professional programme (having completed an undergraduate programme), your undergraduate marks must be above average and, except in rare cases, you will be required to sit a standardised exam such as the LSAT (law), the MCAT (medicine), the GMAT (business) and the GRE (graduate school). They are marked on a percentile basis so that you are judged in comparison with those who sit the exam in the same year.

The college system

Colleges have been going through a boom time lately. Promising jobs, they have been able to compete with universities because they offer more specialised and practical training geared to the job market. There are close to 150 community colleges and institutes in Canada, all members of the Association of Canadian Community Colleges (ACCC). You will hear community colleges called by many names:

- colleges of applied arts and technology
- institutes of applied arts and sciences
- community colleges
- technical/vocational colleges
- institutes of technology or technical institutes.

Each institution has its own entrance requirements and methods of assessing candidates. In most cases these institutions offer diplomas, not degrees. In recent years many university graduates have gone on to a college in order to specialise in an area and become more 'hireable'. At the same time, students in colleges sometimes wish to transfer to a university. This is possible but not for all universities or all programmes. Most college programmes cost significantly less than study at university does.

Colleges' main objective is vocational training through hands-on training. Becoming licensed in a trade involves apprentice work, classroom work and the passing of a provincial examination. Some schools run programmes like universities, that is for eight months of the year, while others go straight through the summer for 12 months in order to accelerate a student's ability to get his or her diploma. The range of courses and programmes is immense. Colleges offer everything from radio and television arts to computer programming, hairdressing, computer animation, carpentry and business administration. Most also offer continuing educational courses that run for a few months (at night) and are open to anyone with an interest and the money for the fee (usually a few hundred dollars).

Chiropractic and naturopathic colleges

There are two special types of colleges that should be discussed separately. Chiropractic College, of which there are only two (one English and one French), is in a field of its own. It is very competitive to get in, requiring a university science degree and good marks. It is also much costlier as it is not subsidised by the government. You can get student loans, but $16,000 plus in yearly tuition is still a steep order. It is a four-year programme with the last year-and-a-half running through the summer months. At the end, graduates become doctors of chiropractic medicine, but are not considered medical doctors (MDs). Falling into a similar category is the Canadian College of Naturopathic Medicine in Toronto. Graduates of this four-year programme become doctors of naturopathic medicine. Tuition is in the same price range as for the chiropractic colleges.

Correspondence courses

A growing field is correspondence education. For those who cannot afford to go away to school or who want to do their education on the side while they continue in their job, some universities and colleges offer courses by correspondence. This involves self-instruction with the aid of textbooks and the mailing in, or emailing of written assignments. Of course, the Internet has really boosted this type of 'distance' learning with audio and visual capabilities so students can observe a class or tutorial from home.

Women in higher education

More than 55 per cent of all university students are now women and more women graduate from university than do men. More and more, women are finding that the best way to break through the 'glass ceiling' is to be better educated and accredited than their male counterparts. The same can be seen in college figures where more than 53 per cent of full-time college students and nearly 63 per cent of part-time college students are women. These figures apply to all types of programmes, including formerly male-dominated ones like medicine.

Student safety

Partly because of the increased presence of women at universities, and partly because of the growth of universities both in number of students and size of campus, student safety has become a huge issue at universities and colleges. Large universities often have their own police stations on campus and there are walk-home programmes run by student volunteers for anyone wanting an escort home after dark. Campus pay phones are equipped with special emergency buttons, parking lots are well lit and crisis hotlines have been set up. Campus crime still exists, but these measures have ensured that they are as safe as possible.

FOREIGN STUDENTS

A foreign student is not one who has come as a refugee or a landed immigrant. Foreign students are those visiting Canada on a student visa. As a foreign student, you may go to Canada to study as an exchange student or you may go having organised it on your own.

Canadian universities covet foreign students and often boast of the percentage attending their school. This is because foreign students add prestige to a university, and also because they have to pay more tuition. You may want to study abroad because to have a year or more of education at a foreign university that is well recognised by the international community can be an asset when it comes time to look for a job. You may desire a year of study in Canada as a trial run to determine whether Canada is a country you may want to live in permanently. In addition to this chapter, there is more information about student visas in Chapter 3.

Tuition

The downside is that tuition fees for foreign students are much higher because the government does not subsidise education for foreigners. So while a Canadian student pays $4,000 for a year in a liberal arts programme, a foreign student may pay more than double that, sometimes three times as much. This is part of the reason universities covet foreign students. Unfortunately, foreign students are not eligible for provincial or national student loans or bursaries. However, some universities have scholarships especially for international students, and although it varies from university to university, after a year of study international students may be eligible for in-course scholarships which are based on the previous year of study.

Applying to a Canadian university, for the most part, works the same for foreign students as it does for Canadians and permanent residents.

Visas

You do not need a study permit if your studies are in a short-term programme of six months or less. But if you think you might want to extend your studies or do another programme afterwards, it's wise to get the permit before coming to Canada. Then, you can apply to study the new programme from within Canada, rather than having to leave and apply again from abroad. If you are from the USA, Greenland, or Saint Pierre and Miquelon, you can apply at a port of entry when you arrive at the Canadian border.

Getting a student visa involves a certain amount of paperwork hassle, but as long as you satisfy the requirements, you're on your way to studying in Canada. To apply for a **student permit** you need to:

- have a valid passport
- have a letter of acceptance from the educational institution
- have enough money to support yourself (tuition, living expenses and money for transport home)
- proof that you will return home at the end of your studies
- complete an application form
- pay the $125 fee.

Depending on what country you are from, you may even need to get a visitor's visa in addition to the student permit, as well as a medical examination. Check with the Canadian Embassy or consulate in your country to find out whether this is necessary for you or not.

Before going any further, it's important to note that some courses of study do not require a student visa. Those are:

- an English or French language course that lasts a maximum of three months

- non-academic, professional or vocational studies such as:
    - self-improvement, general interest courses such as arts and crafts
    - courses included in tour packages as a secondary activity for tourists
    - day care or nursery school programmes that are not a compulsory part of the elementary school system.

You have to get your student permit before leaving to study in Canada. There are a few exceptions to this rule, but again, the nearest Canadian visa office is where to check for the most up-to-date information. There are also helpful foreign student guides on

Immigration and Citizenship Canada website (see Useful Addresses).

The **letter of acceptance** from the educational institution is imperative. The college or university will decide if you meet its academic and language requirements and, therefore, you have to deal directly with the school itself.

If you are planning to study in the province of Quebec, you must apply directly to a Quebec Immigration Service Office to get both your visa and obtain a Certificat d'acceptation du Quebec (Quebec Certificate of Acceptance or CAQ). QIS offices serve citizens of France, Monaco, Austria, Lebanon, Syria, Mexico and Hong Kong. If you are a citizen of any other country, applications are made to the regional office covering the territory in which the educational institution is located, or for the Montreal area, to the 'Direction des services de l'immigration sociale et humanitaire'.

Again, there are exceptions that mean you do not have to apply for a CAQ. For more information and for addresses and phone numbers for all of the above types of offices, check Quebec's immigration website (see Useful Addresses). You can also get information at your local Canadian consular office.

You must not have a criminal record. If you decide to change schools or your course of studies, you will have to reapply to the new educational institution and for another student visa but you can do so from within Canada.

Health insurance

Canada does not cover medical costs of foreign students. In some cases, the educational institution itself will have a health insurance programme for foreign students, with the premium included in their student fees (however it's not cheap, often about $500). Some of those plans cover dental insurance, some don't. But if the university does have such a plan, it is compulsory to enrol unless you can prove you have cover with another insurer.

If the province does have cover, universities can often provide additional cover for medication, ambulances and dental work. The provinces that do have some form of health care cover for foreign students are:

◆ British Columbia: three-month waiting period before you are covered by the B.C. Medical Plan and the B.C. Hospital Insurance Plan. Must have own insurance for that time. Study period must last more than six months. $36/month for a single student. After 12 months, you can apply for premium assistance, and therefore not have to pay full fees. Medical services must be contacted if you're out of the province for more than two months.

◆ Alberta: the Alberta Health Care Insurance Plan covers foreign students on study permits that will last at least 12 months. Single student costs $34 a month.

◆ Saskatchewan: apply and register through the International Student Office. A card will be issued within a month. Optometrists, dentists, medication and ambulances not covered. No charge for cover. Conditions that apply are arrival in Saskatchewan directly from your country of origin and not having been in another Canadian province for longer than three months.

◆ Manitoba: covered from first day of arrival in province. Annual
cost is $453 for a single student, as long as the proposed plan of
study is for more than six months. You pay the fee to the
university along with tuition. The university then pays the
province.

◆ Quebec: only if you work in province (on-campus work included)
can you apply for the Quebec Medicare.

◆ Nova Scotia: you can apply to enrol in the provincial plan if you
are in the province for more than 13 months and are not absent
for more than 31 days that whole time. Cover doesn't begin until
the first day of your 13th month, so you are responsible for your
own insurance for the first 12 months.

In the case of the above provinces, even though they allow cover
under their health plans, it is probably a good idea to get travel
insurance for when you first arrive to cover the first few days,
weeks, or months of your stay.

Exchanges

There are formal exchange programmes orchestrated by non-
governmental organisations (NGOs) but the majority of student
exchanges are done by the individual institutions. If you know
where you would like to study, contact the schools in that province
or city and see what exchange programmes they offer. Check with
your own university or college to see if it has any special
agreements with particular schools in Canada.

Working

Foreign students are now allowed to work while in Canada. First,
if the work is an essential and integral part of your study, it is
allowed. This does not include accountants, medical interns and

medical residents. It is permitted if it is related to an approved research or training programme. International full-time students can work at jobs that are on the campus of the school they attend. Canadian universities and colleges have student centres, athletic centres, bars and restaurants on campus that provide employment opportunities for students. Students can work off-campus for up to 20 hours per week during academic sessions, and full time during scheduled breaks. Students have to apply for a work permit to do so, however, and they have to be enrolled at a participating institution. See www.cic.gc.ca for a list of such institutions. Once you finish your study in Canada, you can work for up to one year in a related field.

See Chapters 3 and 7 for more about work permits.

9

Driving in Canada

Driving in Canada can be both a pleasure and a challenge. For people from smaller countries, it can be quite an adjustment to drive in a country that spans six time zones. Canadians won't think twice about driving for hours to a destination for a mere weekend away – or even just for day excursions. With long, open roads and often spectacular scenery, driving in Canada can be a liberating and magnificent feeling. At the same time, city driving can be anything but liberating and remaining patient is not easy for anyone, not just newly arrived immigrants and visitors. Knowing what to expect can go a long way to making the whole experience a lot easier.

PROVINCE TO PROVINCE

Canada's roads are fairly decent, although the ice and snow in the winter and heat and humidity in the summer can wreak havoc on the roads of some of the most populous cities which is why there are always ongoing roadworks. City roads are fairly wide since most cities were planned for automobiles, not like the more historic cities of Europe. Cities like Quebec City and parts of Halifax are exceptions to this. Most roads are well marked, although if you don't read French, you may have difficulty in Quebec where French-only signs exist.

City driving

If you come from a big city like London, New York, New Delhi
or Sydney, you may find cities like Toronto or Vancouver quite
tame, but by Canadian standards traffic in big cities is chaotic
and every year it seems to get worse. However, most cities are
planned on a grid system, which makes them fairly easy to
navigate. At the same time, downtown sections are usually made
up of many one-way streets to help with traffic flow, which can see
even the best navigators end up going in circles. Roundabouts are,
for the most part, novel entities. Since most streets run north,
south, east and west, junctions are controlled by traffic lights.
Rush hour (from about 7am to 9am, and 4pm to 6pm) is to be
dreaded, especially when there are road closures due to perpetual
repairs. People can get into bad tempers, but there are relatively
few cases of real 'road rage' in Canada. Some cities, such as
Toronto, are busy at all hours except the very early morning.
Montreal is known for its daring and aggressive drivers.

Rural driving

Some country driving, like that in the Prairies, is flat, straight and
very boring, but in other parts roads can wind endlessly. Either
way, it's important to pay attention and stay alert. Wildlife, poor
visibility and other sleepy drivers can make rural roads treacherous.
On gravel roads you need to be aware of dust and flying stones
from other cars and trucks. One of the most important things is to
try not to drive longer distances than you can manage in a short
period of time, especially at night. You may be eager to get
somewhere, but many drivers get into trouble when they ignore
their increasing drowsiness.

Travelling on highways and freeways

The main routes in and out of the big cities are usually high-speed, multi-lane freeways (also called expressways or highways). In Britain such routes are called motorways and in mainland Europe they are known as autobahns, autoroutes and autostradas. A few of Canada's expressways charge a toll, the incentive to use them being less traffic. Most major arteries are well lit.

Linking towns and cities across Canada are highways that stretch for miles and miles. The recently upgraded ones near cities have three to four lanes on either side, but once you get to more rural areas there is usually only one lane on either side, sometimes with the odd passing section when it expands to two lanes for a short distance.

Canada has about 24,500 km of highways. The **Trans Canada Highway**, which runs from St John's, Newfoundland to Victoria, British Columbia, is a whopping 7,306 km, the longest in the world. Along most main highways are service stations that include one or more restaurants, rest room facilities and a gas (petrol) station. But for driving in more out-of-the-way areas drivers are advised to bring extra gasoline, food, water, warm clothing in winter and a cellular phone. Music tapes or CDs could also be useful for when you are travelling in rural areas where radio station options are limited.

Deer crossing

In some areas, alongside the usual road signs warning of sharp bends or rock avalanches, there are signs alerting drivers to beware of certain wildlife that roams nearby. It's not just to protect the animals; deer, elk and moose can be a real hazard for cars and their drivers. They often get mesmerised by car lights and stand frozen in the path of your car, or can bolt across the road out of nowhere. If you hit one of these large animals, especially a moose, you can be killed. Smaller animals like racoon, squirrels or skunks aren't a danger, but you won't enjoy the smell if you hit them, and it's never nice to think you've killed an animal.

KNOWING THE RULES OF THE ROAD

In contrast to the other Commonwealth countries, Canadians drive on the right-hand side. That means that the lane to the right is the slowest and the one on the left is the passing lane. Seatbelt-wearing is compulsory throughout the country. Some rules vary from province to province and you will need to familiarise yourself with the particular rules of the province you're staying in. For example, Quebec is the only province in which it is illegal to make a right-hand turn on a red light.

Each province enforces a point system whereby certain driving offences result in the loss of a specified amount of points from a base amount. If a driver has lost a large amount of points, he or she may be called in for an interview or may get his or her licence suspended automatically. When a driver loses all his or her points, the licence is usually taken away for a certain period of time.

Keeping to speed limits

Speeding is a big problem in Canada where impatient drivers take advantage of the wide, open roads. There have been numerous graphic advertising campaigns launched as an attempt to point out the tragic results of speeding. Nevertheless, it continues to happen and there are stiff fines for those who are caught. If you are used to the imperial system, it might take some time to get used to the metric system employed in Canada. Don't make the mistake of interpreting a sign that says '90' to mean 90 mph! The speed limit on highways is usually 100 km/h (60 mph) and in cities and towns it is usually 40–50 km/h (25–30 mph) or less.

Drunk-driving

Drunk-driving, called drink-driving in countries such as Britain and Australia, is a serious offence. The legal blood-alcohol limit is 0.08, or 80 milligrams of alcohol per 100 milligrams of blood. If you're caught with more than that while driving, you have committed a criminal offence that can lead to licence suspension, hefty fines and even jail. Killing someone while driving when drunk is considered a form of murder and carries with it a maximum jail sentence of 14 years. However, it should also be noted, that while it's not a criminal offence, having a blood-alcohol count of more than 0.05 (and less than 0.08) will also be punished with sanctions, such as licence suspension and/or fine.

One method of catching impaired drivers is random breath testing. It is an offence to refuse a breathalyser test. Some provinces have graduated licensing so that in the first year of driving there is a zero tolerance policy – a driver caught with a higher than 0.0 level will end up with a suspended licence for a prescribed period of time. This policy is an attempt to deter younger people from driving under the influence of alcohol since a leading cause of death of teenagers is car accidents.

Making way for pedestrians

Unlike in some countries, where at unmarked crossways pedestrians run hurriedly to get out of a car's way, Canadians take their time crossing a road. It's not because they're trying to provoke you; it's because pedestrians have the right of way – everywhere. So even though jay walking is illegal, if you hit a person who is doing so you're in big trouble. There used to be an advertising campaign aimed at pedestrians that said, 'You're right: Dead right' in an attempt to emphasise that people should not be careless when crossing just because it's a car's duty to stop. As in many countries, in Canada there is special signage to indicate when children, the elderly and the blind might be crossing, so that drivers take extra care. Another thing to note is that when a stationary school bus has its red lights flashing, you must stop regardless of what direction you are driving. The flashing lights mean children are getting on and off.

DRIVERS' LICENCES

Regulations vary from province to province in terms of how long a driver can drive on a valid foreign licence before having to seek a local licence. This time period is usually 90 to 120 days for a new resident. As a tourist, however, this period of grace is usually the full six months, because a tourist visa is temporary. You can also obtain an International Driver's Permit from your home country that is valid for one year.

When it comes time to get a local licence, it varies from province to province in terms of the requirements. Provinces such as Ontario, Quebec and Prince Edward Island have graduated licensing which means there are different levels of licences. A lower level licence is the first stage for a new driver and usually includes restrictions on night driving and/or blood-alcohol limits. Once a driver passes that level, he or she takes the test for the next level and eventually becomes a fully entitled driver. There are fees involved at all testing stages of these licensing programmes.

Some provinces do not require any re-testing and you can make a direct exchange with your foreign licence for a local one, although there may be an age requirement or you might have to have a certain number of years' driving experience. Some provinces require both written and road tests and the amount of provable driving experience you have will determine at what level you begin your testing (i.e. in the graduated licensing programmes). Licences are usually good for three to five years and renewing it only requires a fee and a new photo being taken, not a re-test of the driver road exam. However, if a licence is left to lapse, a new written and road test is required.

Each province has its own ministry of transport that can provide information on that province's requirements and advise you on your own particular situation.

OWNING A CAR

In 2006 there were 20.1 million registered motor vehicles in Canada. The main cities have public transport systems, but many people feel a car is necessary for travelling longer distances, especially if they live in the suburbs or a rural area.

Buy it in Canada or bring your own?

There are stiff restrictions on foreign cars (those made outside either Canada or the US), so you may find it completely impractical or even impossible to import your own. According to the **Motor Vehicle Safety Act and Regulations**, all vehicles imported into Canada must comply with Canadian safety standards. For the most part, foreign cars do not comply and cannot be modified to comply. This is not a case of the driver's side being opposite to those in Canada; that is not an issue. Usually it comes down to something like the seatbelt anchorage point being in the wrong place. Cars older than a *full* 15 years are exempt from this law, as are buses manufactured before 1 January 1971. Cars bought in the United States can often be modified, if necessary, to meet Canadian safety standards unless they have been already altered to fit another country's requirements. Vehicles that have been designed, built, tested and certified to meet either all of Canada's standards or all US standards might be allowed in if they come with a 'statement of compliance' label affixed by the original manufacturer (as long as the car has not been altered since it was made and the manufacturer's certification has been maintained).

Visitors and tourists, however, can bring in a motor vehicle temporarily without complying with the Canadian safety regulations as long as the car is used exclusively by a person who is a visitor or a person passing through Canada to another country. People who are coming to Canada on a work permit or student visa are considered visitors in this regard. You can't, however, sell or dispose of such a vehicle while in Canada.

Even if your car meets the requirements, it must go through customs and is subject to duty, which may be more expensive than you think. Servicing a foreign car can be costly because of the lack of parts. To determine the suitability of your car contact Transport Canada (see Useful Addresses).

Buying new
If you come from a country with a currency that trades strongly against the Canadian dollar, buying in Canada might be a good idea. The recent surge in the Canadian dollar against the American dollar, however, has lured some people to buy in the US and import into Canada. Even with duties and the cost of modifications, some vehicles are still cheaper if bought south of the border.

Prices in Canada range widely depending on the brand and features of the car. Lowest prices for a new car are around $12,000 for something like a small hatchback. Mid-size cars are usually in the $20,000 to $40,000 range. Top-end cars are pricey to buy and to take care of. Right now, sport utility vehicles (SUVs) are all the rage, even though their sturdiness is not necessary in the city – and it comes with a price too. SUVs are also gas guzzlers, which is bad for the wallet and for the environment.

Buying used
Buying a used vehicle is also an option. Auto trading magazines and the classified advertising sections of the newspapers are the best places to search. New car dealers also sell used cars, although the increase in accountability of a dealer usually comes at a higher price. The advantage of a used car is that the major portion of

depreciation has already taken place, but you may end up sacrificing having a warranty in the process. It's extremely important that you get a qualified mechanic to check the car to ensure it's not a money pit waiting to happen.

Leasing

Leasing-to-own is one of the most popular options now because many people can't commit to buying a car outright. A deposit of a few thousand dollars is usually required and then a monthly payment is agreed upon, with interest. After a certain period of time you have the option of buying the car by paying the remainder of the price or trading in the car for another, newer car (and getting a new lease). The downside to leasing is if you cannot afford to buy it, or choose not to buy the car, when your option to do so comes up, the deposit and monthly payments are lost money. However, because leasing is so popular, dealership competition means that there are some very cheap leases that make economical sense. And for those who own their own business and use the car mostly for that business, lease payments can be used as an income tax deduction (as a business expense).

Things to take into account

Remember that cars have a shorter life span in Canada because of salt put on the roads in the winter. Rust can develop before you know it. Cars last longer on the mild West Coast. You will probably have to invest in a pair of winter tyres or at least some all-season radials. In the coldest regions you may have to 'plug in' your car overnight to prevent it from freezing up. The device is called a block heater and can be purchased and installed at most repair garages.

Finally, Ontario has a 'drive clean' programme that began in Toronto and Hamilton and has now expanded to south western and eastern Ontario. The programme requires an emission test every two years. If your car fails, you must pay for whatever service repairs are needed to get your emissions to a prescribed limit.

INSURING AND REGISTERING

Insurance is mandatory. As a foreigner (unless you are American) you will be considered an inexperienced driver unless you can prove your driving experience or there is a reciprocal agreement between the province and your country (e.g. Ontario and Japan). Insurance rates are highest for inexperienced drivers, drivers under 25 and in general young male drivers. Rates are also dependent on the age and make of the car, and the city you live in (major metropolitan areas are more expensive than smaller cities). The cost of insurance ranges widely, but generally you're looking at $880 to $2,500 a year.

Registration with the provincial registry of motor vehicles office is also mandatory and includes an annual fee of $53 to more than $255 depending on the province, and the city in which you live.

JOINING MOTOR ASSOCIATIONS

The Canadian Automobile Association (CAA) provides 24-hour emergency roadside assistance for any trouble you may have from locking your keys in the car to a flat tyre or complete breakdown. Many people find the annual membership fee (ranging from $55 for basic services to $120 for premium services) worth the money, especially if they own an older car or drive long distances.

Some car dealers offer their own roadside assistance as part of the sale package.

GASOLINE

Also known as petrol in Europe, gasoline (gas – or gaz in Quebec) varies in price across the country. You'll find higher prices in the far north and the east, especially in Quebec. Prices often inexplicably rise before weekends and holidays and you will see this noted in newspapers from time to time. Gasoline is sold by the litre.

Despite heavy competition between gasoline companies, price wars are rare. In fact, at an intersection with two competing stations, the prices are likely to be close if not identical and to rise and fall together. Most stations are self-serve but there are full-serve options as well.

USING OTHER TRANSPORT

As mentioned before, major cities have some form of public transport, such as buses, streetcars (trams), light rail and underground train systems. Montreal and Toronto are the only ones with underground trains, called the Metro in Montreal and the Subway in Toronto. They also have commuter trains serving the suburbs and outer regions. If you live in the city core, you may not need a vehicle; for longer trips there's the option of renting a car.

For long-distance travel Canada has a bus system, such as Greyhound or Voyageur Colonial, that serves major centres as well as some rural ones. A bit more expensive but faster is VIA Rail that connects major centres across Canada. Even pricier is flying, although it's also the most common method of travel for long distance in Canada, since the country is so big.

Canada has one major and several smaller airlines. The industry in Canada has been in turmoil over the last few years. Canada's second major airline, Canadian Airlines went bankrupt and was taken over by Air Canada – now the country's only national airline serving major and minor centres in Canada and the US and major cities worldwide. However, Air Canada recently emerged from bankruptcy protection, which shows how vulnerable airlines can be.

Canada 3000, formerly Canada's biggest charter airline, went bankrupt after the September 11 terrorist attacks in the US. Since then, domestic discount carrier JetsGo also went under. Can Jet recently downgraded itself from a scheduled airline to a charter airline.

On the flipside, a new airline called Zoom started up flights from some Canadian cities to Glasgow, London, Belfast, Manchester, Cardiff and Paris. And newcomer Porter Airlines goes between Toronto, Ottawa, Montreal and Halifax. And then there's Air Transat, a well-established charter airline specialising in holiday packages.

Domestically, Air Canada's biggest competitor is West Jet, which started in the west but has rapidly expanded to serve many cities in Canada and the US. Of course, there are also small, regional airlines such as Bearskin Airlines and Central Mountain Air. Even with competition, airfares are not as cheap as they are in the UK, Europe or Australia. Beware: a flight from Toronto to Vancouver can cost as much or more than one from Toronto to the UK.

Not unlike elsewhere in the world, the September 11 attacks led to tighter security at airports and other ports of entry to Canada. To pay for higher security costs at airports, the Canadian government has instituted a $24 round-trip security fee for all passengers. Due to complaints that this is exorbitant, the government has responded by lowering the fee gradually since then. The security charge on a domestic round trip flight is $9.90, a transborder flight is $8.42 and an international flight is $17.00.

Because Canada has so many bodies of water within its boundaries and on three of its borders, marine travel is by no means obsolete. Because of the islands on the West and East Coasts, ferries and cruises are particularly popular there.

Having Fun

After a long winter Canadians like to make the most of their summers by enjoying activities in the great outdoors. With such ready access to nature, Canadians are blessed with a multitude of choices. And even though hibernation in winter is a cosy prospect, six or more months of colder weather is not enough to stop a real Canuck from playing outdoors. Some 4.4 million Canadians, 15 years or older, participate in organised or club sports. Arts and cultural events are alive and well too. When it comes to relaxing and kicking back, Canadians have some unique ways of doing so.

ENJOYING SPORTS AND RECREATION

You don't have to be an Olympic athlete to enjoy sports in Canada. With so much nature right at the doorstep, all you need to do is step outside. There are fun, recreational and competitive leagues for any sport you can think of. Schools have physical education classes as well as sports teams, universities have recreational and competitive teams and many companies have office teams. Canada has had its share of shame with doping scandals, but it has also been a leader in the fight against doping in sport. It is ranked among the top 15 countries as a sporting nation.

Canada has hosted almost every major international sporting competition: the Summer and Winter Olympics, Commonwealth

Games, Pan-American Games and World University Games and FIFA Under-20 World Cup.

Ice and snow

When most people think of winter sport in Canada they think of hockey. Although lacrosse is Canada's official national sport, hockey is by far the favourite spectator sport and one that is played recreationally by kids and adults alike. More than 450,000 young people participate in organised hockey leagues and many more play on frozen lakes, outdoor rinks and in the streets.

Hockey is not the only winter sporting activity. There's also ice-skating, speed-skating, figure-skating, tobogganing, ice-climbing, downhill-skiing, cross-country skiing and curling, to name a few.

Spring, summer, autumn

Many people probably don't even think of warm weather when they think of Canada, but if you ask Canadians what some of their favourite sport activities are they will cite swimming, baseball, tennis and track. Granted most outdoor sports can be, and are, accommodated indoors, but when Canadians can play them outside, they will. Some favourites, other than those mentioned already, are: soccer (European football), field hockey, lacrosse, basketball, triathlon, rock climbing, surfing, sailing, cycling, hiking, ultimate frisbee, golf, rugby, football (Canadian style) and horseback riding.

Summer days seem especially and wonderfully long because of daylight savings time. On the second Sunday in March, everyone (except for most of Saskatchewan) sets their clocks forward by one hour. It has the effect of making the daylight stretch well into the evening in the summertime and makes it perfect for outdoor activities. However, in the autumn (from the first Sunday in November), the clocks go back by an hour again.

Participating in amateur and professional sport

Olympics

Every four years Canada sends its best athletes to the Olympics. Canadians have excelled in sports like figure skating and skiing, but you may be surprised to learn that it is a leader in synchronised swimming, rowing and horse show jumping as well. Unfortunately, like in the UK, athletes and their coaches have long complained of underfunding and a lack of support from the government.

Canada has hosted a few Olympics, the most recent being the 1988 Winter Games in Calgary. Vancouver will serve as host for the 2010 Winter Olympics.

Hockey

Canada has six teams in the National Hockey League (NHL): Vancouver, Calgary, Edmonton, Toronto, Ottawa and Montreal. There used to be teams for Winnipeg and Quebec City, but monetary problems drove those teams to move to the United States. In fact, when the Colorado Avalanche, which used to be the Quebec Nordiques, first moved to Colorado, most of the names on the back of the players' jerseys were French.

In coming to Canada, it is important that you understand how entrenched hockey is in the psyche of Canadians. Even those who are not fans feel possessive of it as a Canadian sport. Canadians aren't well known as nationalists, except when it comes to hockey. It has been difficult for Canadians to see teams proliferating in the US as the Canadian teams struggle because of expanding player salaries and a low Canadian dollar. When Canadian hockey hero Wayne Gretzky retired from the sport in April 1999, it was a day of mourning for Canadians, even though he played most of his career for American teams. In fact, the day in 1988 when he was first traded to an American team from the Edmonton Oilers is called 'The day Canada stood still'.

However, Canada's hockey confidence was given a huge boost recently when in the 2002 Winter Olympics in Salt Lake City, both the women's and men's hockey teams won gold against the US teams. Canadians, ignoring cold temperatures, spilled out into the streets of every city across the country in celebration. In 2006, the women's team won gold again at the games in Turin.

Although there are more American teams than Canadian ones, the majority of NHL players are Canadian. The NHL hockey season runs from October to June when it concludes with the playoffs for the Stanley Cup, a trophy symbolising hockey supremacy in North America.

In addition to Olympic competition, international competitions include the World Junior Championships, the World Championships and the Canada Cup.

Basketball

Not many people know it was a Canadian who invented basketball, especially as it remains a sport dominated by Americans through the National Basketball Association (NBA).

Canada has only one NBA team, the Toronto Raptors. Its Vancouver team, the Grizzlies, recently moved to Memphis due to financial woes (and poor fan turnout). The Raptors are relatively popular, even if they haven't fared all that well in the standings. The basketball season runs roughly parallel to the hockey season, also culminating in a playoff championship series.

Soccer

While Canadians don't go nearly as mad for soccer as Europeans do, it is gaining popularity, both for women and men. The 2002 FIFA Women's World Cup for under 19-year-olds was held in Edmonton and attracted record crowds, more than 25,000 people at some games. The Canadian team won silver. In the summer of 2007, several Canadian cities hosted the men's FIFA Under-20 World Cup. FIFA considered it one of its most successful tournaments ever with most games selling out.

Canada's women's team fares quite well internationally, but the men's national team rarely qualifies for the high profile FIFA World Cup tournament. That's probably why Canada's best players continue to play in Europe rather than at home. In fact, Canada's most famous soccer export, Owen Hargreaves, plays for England thanks to dual citizenship.

However, soccer is one of the most popular sports for both boys and girls to play recreationally in Canada.

Football

Football in Canada is not what's called football in the rest of the world – that is soccer to Canadians. Football is the game with the oval-shaped dark leather ball being thrown about by individuals sporting massive padded equipment. In Canada the US-style game is played with a few modifications. The Canadian Football League (CFL) began as a league of only Canadian teams, and then managed to expand to include a couple of American ones. But now it's back to an all-Canadian line-up of teams. Canadian teams include Calgary, Edmonton, Regina, Hamilton, Montreal, Vancouver, Toronto and Winnipeg. They play for the Grey Cup at the end of the season.

Baseball

Again, this is an American dominated sport, but Canada does have two teams, one in Montreal and one in Toronto. However, the Montreal Expos are slated to be cut from Major League Baseball in a couple of years, as the league sets to contract rather than expand. The season begins in the spring and ends in October with the World Series championship. The name of the championship is a bit of a misnomer as the series is just North American. In 1992 and 1993 the Toronto Blue Jays won the World Series causing pandemonium in Toronto and even a trickle in the rest of Canada.

OUTDOOR RECREATION

Canada's geography lends itself naturally to 'outdoor rec'. Camping, both in summer and in winter, is a popular activity, especially for family trips. Canoeing is also a national pastime with its Native Indian roots. Even fishing can be done all year round. In the winter people go out on frozen lakes, place a wooden hut on the ice, drill a hole or two in the ice and cast a rod in the water. Such is the ritual of ice fishing. In the summer, fishing is a little bit more accessible. Canada is covered with walking and hiking trails. In fact, in the works is a project to build a continuous trail from one end of the country to the other.

It's called the Trans Canada Trail and once completed it will be the longest recreational trail in the world, at almost 18,000 kilometres. It is being built by linking existing trails with new construction. It is projected that the trail will be 'substantially complete' by the autumn of 2010.

When you come to Canada you will hear a lot about 'cottage country'. It is quite popular to go 'up north' or 'to the country' in the summer and even the winter for one's vacation.

There, people either own or rent cottages (also called cabins, camps or lodges in different parts of Canada) that range from rustic accommodation to glamorous getaways. Often small towns that are relatively quiet most of the year come alive in the summer months, although some cottages are winterised and used all year. These towns are usually near a lake and outdoor recreation is centred on water sports like water skiing, boating, jet skiing, swimming and fishing. Hunting in some areas is also popular, and is allowed under certain conditions.

Dangers – or not really

Canada is fairly safe for those who like to spend their time outdoors, but there are things that you should be aware of. In terms of diseases, rabies has not yet been wiped out in Canada, although incidence rates are low and no human has ever died from rabies in Canada. The West Nile virus, a mosquito-borne disease, has now crept into Canada from the US, having been found in animals (mostly birds) in every province but PEI and Newfoundland/Labrador. At the height of the crisis, in the summer of 2003, there were almost 1,500 human cases with the majority in Saskatchewan, Ontario, Alberta and Manitoba. In

2006, there were 151 human cases and in 2007, up to the beginning of August, there were only 25 cases, all in Manitoba. Health officials credit better surveillance, pesticide and public education programmes for the marked decrease. To date 36 people have died from West Nile Virus in Canada.

On a less serious note, in the spring pesky black flies can drive you mad. They are tiny flies that bite, you don't feel it but you do bleed a bit. They also, annoyingly, get caught in your hair. Mosquitoes are probably more annoying because their bite itches and there's nothing worse than when you are camping and nearly asleep and you hear a faint buzzing around your ear. Then you know a mosquito is about to strike.

Aside from the above and from the odd bumble bee or sand gnat, there is not much to worry about regarding stings and bites as Canada has no poisonous spiders or insects. Canada does have the rattlesnake, which is poisonous, in Ontario, Alberta and British Columbia, but bites are rare (they're shy animals) and anti-venom treatment is available.

When people first come to Canada, they seem to worry a lot about bears. It's very unlikely you will see a bear in a major city. Bears usually live in wild areas. But, if you go camping in a National Park or live in the north, near forests or mountains, precautions are necessary. Keeping food sealed and stored away from where you sleep (tent, cabin etc.) and suspended high off a tree branch is the best idea. Whatever you do, don't feed them or try to get close-up photos of them and especially stay away from a mommy bear's cubs!

Other than that, there are just the pesky squirrels, racoons and mice. Don't feed them either and again, store food securely.

In the winter there's very little to bother the outdoor enthusiast, no matter what you hear about wolves and polar bears. It's highly unlikely you'll be camping anywhere near where they live.

Exploring National Parks

Thirty-seven National Parks exist in Canada in an attempt to protect and preserve the unique flora and fauna in those areas. As this book is written, there are plans to create more. Camping is allowed and sometimes canoes can be rented. Park entrance fees vary from park to park. Banff is the oldest National Park, having opened in 1885. The most popular are probably Jasper, Banff, Cape Breton Highlands, Pacific Rim and the Rocky Mountain parks. Each province also runs its own system of parks.

Going to summer camp

A favourite pastime for Canadian children is to go to 'camp'. Some are specialised, such as equestrian, arts and crafts, gymnastics or sailing. Others are general outdoors camps that include canoe trips, arts and crafts, hiking, woodcrafts and swimming. Many of the general outdoors camps are girls-only or boys-only and most are sleepover camps where the kids stay overnight for a week or more.

Camps vary widely in terms of cost; the stay-away camps are usually the priciest. Kids who go back every summer sometimes opt to be counsellors in training (CITs) and then fully-fledged counsellors, but the pay is not outstanding (however, the leadership training is).

There are camps in the city, just outside the city and ones far, far away. There are day camps, overnight camps and camps for children with special needs. There are special camps for children from low-income families who otherwise would not be able to afford to go. Essentially, there is a camp for anyone who wants to go.

Patio time

It's pushing it a little to include patio culture under outdoor recreation, but Canadians like to think of it as such. Although Canada sees more cold than warm, its cafés, restaurants and bars are well equipped with patios for the summer months. Canadians don't always wait until the summer to put them in use. As soon as the sun comes out and the snow starts melting, desperate Canucks will don whatever will keep them warm enough to be able to sit outside. When it finally does become warm, patios and sidewalk cafés thrive.

Many houses, and certainly most cottages, have porches, patios, balconies or decks for barbecues, sunbathing and parties. Canadian beer companies have long used fantasy patio culture in their commercials to promote their brand. They show beautiful people gathering in beautiful surroundings having a beautiful time all because of the beer they are drinking.

EXPLORING THE ARTS

Although Canada isn't hundreds of years old, it does have a lot to offer in the way of arts. Because it is so young there is a great deal of modern art and dance, and innovation in film and theatre.

Most of the big cities have the typical fare of big musicals and plays, but smaller, independent productions are offered too. Even smaller towns and rural areas offer some form of theatre and it's often quite good.

Theatre

Many theatres struggle to stay alive monetarily, but nevertheless if you want to see a play there is much to choose from. Mainstream theatre, alternative theatre and large-scale musicals fill the marquees. Prices are across the board, from less than $20 for a play in a warehouse playhouse to $100 or more for a big name musical.

The famous Cirque du Soleil is a circus/theatre troupe that has found international fame with its amazing acrobatics and original acts.

The main theatre season is from November to May but in the summer there are dozens of festivals, both indoor and outdoor. Big cities and small towns alike hold music festivals (blues, jazz, folk, chamber music etc.) or offer theatre-in-the-park in the summertime. And then there are theatre offerings at the famous Stratford or Shaw festivals.

Music

Canadian musicians have done very well on the international stage, although some people don't know they're Canadian and mistake them for American.

Pop/rock/alternative

Okay, Celine Dion is not mistaken for being American very often. She is perhaps Canada's best known export. And maybe Bryan

Adams and Nelly Furtado are known to be Canucks. Less identifiably Canadian are the Barenaked Ladies, Alanis Morissette, Sarah McLachlan, Jann Arden, Sum 41, Nickelback, Avril Lavigne, Kathleen Edwards, Hawksley Wortman, K-OS, Mobile and Our Lady Peace. This list is, of course, in no way exhaustive.

A couple of decades ago, Rush and The Guess Who also made it big. Newcomers arrive on the scene every week and time will tell whether they will be catapulted into fame like former unknown Alanis Morissette or the Barenaked Ladies. There are also names that are huge in Canada but relatively unknown beyond its borders. The Tragically Hip and Blue Rodeo are bands that are very popular with Canadians. They sell out wherever they go.

There are rock concerts all year long, but summer is when the concert season really heats up with outdoor venues and multi-act shows.

Country

Anne Murray is a household name and now Shania Twain is as well, although their interpretations of country music are very different. Country remains less popular in Canada than in the US, but it does continue to garner more fans every year. Other Canadian stars include kd Lang, Rita McNeil and Prairie Oyster.

Folk

This is probably the music for which Canadians are best known. Leonard Cohen, Joni Mitchell, Gordon Lightfoot and Neil Young are known throughout the world. Stars like Sarah McLachlan are lumped under pop music, but many feel her melodies are the 90s version of folk.

Classical/opera/jazz

A number of cities have their own symphony orchestras. The name Glenn Gould is probably the best known among performers of classical music. Classical guitarist Liona Boyd is beloved for her music and voice. Canada might not have its own Vienna, but the Canadian Opera Company is known for the quality of its performances. In terms of jazz, Montreal's annual International Jazz Festival is world-renowned and other cities have followed suit. Canada is quite happy to claim jazz musician Oscar Peterson as its own.

Celtic

Based in the Atlantic Provinces, Celtic music is making a real comeback, as people seem to grow more nostalgic for their Irish and Scottish ancestry. The music is popular throughout the country as the Barra MacNeils, The Rankin Family, Natalie MacMaster and the Irish Descendants bring it a higher profile. Fiddler Ashley McIsaac is quite popular amongst the dance club crowd for marrying the traditional music with a dance beat/sound.

Dance

Modern dance abounds in Canada, but ballet is still a favourite. The National Ballet of Canada has been trying to reinvent itself lately, to mixed reviews, but it, along with the Royal Winnipeg Ballet and the Grands Ballets Canadiens, continues to enjoy international success.

Comedy

Canadians are known for their comedy. It's often joked that with our long winters, we have to have a sense of humour. A long list of Canadian comedians have made it big on the world stage, including Howie Mandel, Mike Myers, Rick Moranis, John

Candy, Martin Short, Dan Ackroyd, Wayne and Schuster, Leslie Nielsen, Catherine O'Hara, Andrea Martin, Colin Mochrie, Jim Carey and Norm MacDonald, to name a few. Shows like *SCTV*, *Kids in the Hall* and *This Hour has 22 Minutes* have launched many of those comedians and others. Through the years, Canadian comedy careers have hit it big on New York's *Saturday Night Live*, and *In Living Colour*. And for the past 25 years, Montreal has hosted one of the biggest comedy festivals in the world: *Just for Laughs*.

Film

Films by the National Film Board seem to be better known outside Canada than within the country. The NFB creates animated, documentary and dramatic films. Canada does have a commercial film industry as well, but compared with the production power of its southern neighbour, Canadian cinema is small and relatively unknown. Some films, however, have become well known and/or internationally critically acclaimed (the two don't necessarily go hand in hand). *My American Cousin*, *Naked Lunch*, *Jesus of Montreal* and *Night Zoo Water,* are well known outside Canadian borders as are many of Atom Egoyan's films (e.g. *The Sweet Hereafter* and *Felicity's Journey*). Unfortunately much of Canada's talent moves south. Director Norman Jewison, who directed such films as *Moonstruck* and *The Hurricane*, works in the United States, although he supports the Canadian industry in a financial and mentoring way. Screenwriter and director Paul Haggis (*Crash*, *Million Dollar Baby*) also works in Holywood. Many actors find more opportunity and money down south after enduring relative anonymity in Canada.

However, many American production companies have preferred filming their productions on Canadian soil due to low production costs and the formerly low Canadian dollar. Both Toronto and Vancouver claim to be the 'Hollywood of the North' and Montreal is becoming popular for US film production too. But the rising Canadian dollar and new incentives south of the border are jeopardising the industry in Canada.

Most of the movies in the cinemas are American, but Canadian and international films can be seen in many of the independent theatres. American movies premiere in Canada at the same time as they first show in the US.

Many cities hold international film festivals. Toronto entertains the largest one, but Vancouver's and Montreal's are well attended too. Most festivals show a few mainstream upcoming movies, but the majority are independent productions that haven't been picked up by a distributor yet. During these festivals the streets are always crammed with limousines and people ogling for the stars to appear.

Native Indian art

Inuit art and Native Indian art are probably among Canada's most recognised art forms. They usually take the form of sculptures and carvings using materials like soapstone, ivory, bone, antler and wood. The subject and style of the art often depends on the geographic region in which the artist lives. Almost all work is done entirely by hand. If you find such art at a cheap price it's most likely a mass-produced copy. Native art can be very expensive.

More reasonably priced and perhaps more practical are the items of clothing the Inuit and Native artists create such as mukluks (moccasins), very thick knitted sweaters and parkas. They also do jewellery, bead work prints and paintings.

Literature

If Canadians are a little insecure about their lack of history when it comes to paintings or their international profile in film, one area where doubt should not exist is that of the writers Canada has produced.

Poetry

Who hasn't heard the poem *In Flanders Fields*? A Canadian soldier, John McCrae, wrote the moving poem in 1915 before he died in the war. Other well known poets are Leonard Cohen, Margaret Atwood and Gwendolyn McEwen. Dennis Lee is renowned for his poetry for children, found in his award-winning book, *Alligator Pie*.

Books

Alice Munro, Margaret Atwood, Robertson Davies, Mordecai Richler, Michael Ondaatje, Margaret Laurence, W O Mitchell, Farley Mowat, Carol Shields, Ann Marie MacDonald, Alistair MacLeod, David Adams Richards, June Callwood, W P Kinsella and Pierre Berton are just a sampling of the Canadian writers who have brought fame and pride to Canadian shores. These authors have written both full-length books and short stories, the later being somewhat of a niche for Canadian writers.

Unfortunately Canadian publishing houses often struggle financially, which has made it difficult for up-and-coming writers to get backing to the same degree the well-established writers did when they started.

Festivals/readings

Promotion of Canadian and international literature is done through book festivals and public readings. Street festivals like Toronto's Word on the Street host all kinds of organisations from mainstream magazine companies to struggling academic journals to freedom of the press advocates. Many bookstores have started up in-house cafes and allow reading there without buying. Also, bookstores, both small and large host authors who read their works and those of others. Universities and independent bookstores also host such readings.

Painting

English and French Canadian artists date back to the 1700s. Much of the art was landscape painting. The Group of Seven was a group of seven artists whose style dominated Canadian art for 30 years (starting from just before WW1). Their work depicted eastern Canada. Emily Carr is also well known for her paintings of the west coast and Native Indian villages and totems. There continue to be many artists who have added to Canada's works, including modern and abstract.

The National Gallery in Ottawa is Canada's premier gallery, but there are art galleries and museums all across the country in major cities and small towns alike.

USING THE MEDIA

Perhaps due to Canada's perpetual inferiority complex or perhaps because of its multiculturalism (or because of both), international news is well covered in Canada. You will be surprised at how in touch with the world you will be. Even though Canadian news isn't front and centre in international papers, Canada does not retaliate in kind. Throughout the last recession, foreign bureaux were scaled back but things are bouncing back now. If you really want to read papers from home there are many news and magazine stores that sell international papers, albeit a day or two late. And, of course, there's always online papers and magazines if you get Internet access.

Newspapers

It's a controversial time for newspapers in Canada, partly because of concentration of ownership and partly because of convergence between print and television. Despite that, readership is at least stable, proving wrong the doomsday calls that the Internet would kill newspapers. But newspapers have embraced the internet, by putting out online versions of their publications and updating them regularly with breaking news. Canada has two national newspapers, the venerable *Globe and Mail* and the nine-year old, *The National Post*. *The Post* was created by former media baron and now British lord, Conrad Black, but he sold it and all his other Canadian dailies and weeklies to the Winnipeg-based Asper family, who also own Global Television.

The Globe is owned by the Thompson family, Torstar (which owns the *Toronto Star* newspaper), the Ontario Teachers' Pension Plan and conglomerate BCE, which owns the Canadian Television Network (CTV). (There are rumours that BCE might sell their media interests in the near future.)

Major cities usually have more than one daily paper to choose from and smaller towns have their own dailies and/or weeklies as well. Alternative, independent weeklies are very popular in the big cities. News coverage is done with a good deal of objectivity, but more and more newspapers are becoming more overt in their ideologies.

Magazines

There are fewer Canadian magazines than there are American ones. Split-run magazines are those which originate in the US but that have some Canadian content, such as the Canadian edition of *Time*. But, Canadian magazines are of a high quality and there is still quite a variety to choose from, although it's hard for them to make money when competing with American magazines. Canada's oldest magazine, *Saturday Night*, is now published only sporadically. However, new magazines do make a go of it from time to time, such as the *Walrus*, a Canadian attempt at its own version of America's *Atlantic Monthly*.

As well, there are many trade, speciality, fashion, news and literary magazines. Some of the mainstream and best-known ones are *Macleans, Flare, Chatelaine, Report on Business* and *Shift*.

Television

The **Canadian Broadcasting Corporation** (CBC) is the publicly-funded broadcaster that has stations all across the country doing national and regional coverage. It is also partly funded by commercials and this has been increasing due to government cutbacks. The Canadian Television Network (CTV), the CBC's main competitor in terms of national coverage, is privately owned, as is the Global Television Network. Global was once upon a time just in southwestern Ontario, but it is now a national broadcaster, although not to the same degree as the CBC or CTV. Both CBC and CTV have 24-hour news channels in addition to their regular channels.

Chum Media has eight local television stations across the country and 17 speciality stations. There are a number of other privately owned local stations across the country. As well, in Ontario, there is also the provincially funded TV Ontario (TVO).

The Canadian Radio, Television and Telecommunications Commission (CRTC) regulates television and radio. It enforces the Canadian content rule to ensure a certain amount of programming is Canadian. This is an incentive for producers to make Canadian shows. Some have turned out to be hits both within Canada and internationally. The big television stations do in-house producing as well.

Shows that have done well that you may have seen in your own country are *The Littlest Hobo*, the *Degrassi* series, *Anne of Green Gables*, *The Road to Avonlea*, *Polka Dot Door*, *Due South*, *Fraggle Rock*, *Kids in the Hall*, *Little Mosque on the Prairie* and *Much Music*. CBC is notorious for its hard-hitting dramas and also well known for its political satire comedy programmes.

However, the Canadian stations do import a great deal of American programming. In addition, Canadians have access through basic cable to many American channels including the main networks, and to North American speciality channels through satellite. Cable is relatively inexpensive compared with European countries. British dramas and sitcoms (Britcoms) are very popular and can be seen on TV Ontario, PBS (the American public broadcasting station), CBC (occasionally) and others. *Coronation Street* and *Eastenders* are both a season or two behind, however.

Canadian television also carries a variety of ethnic and culturally diverse programming and channels. OMNI TV is in BC, Manitoba and Ontario and carries shows in dozens of languages from Albanian, Romanian and Estonian, to Greek and German, to Cantonese and Punjabi. It also broadcasts news in dozens of languages. Digital cable and satellite television providers also offer ethnic channels from back home, whether you speak Arabic, Farsi, Italian, Tamil or one of more than two dozen languages.

Radio
Again, CBC is the national broadcaster on the radio with news, current affairs and music shows that represent all regions of Canada. CBC has both French and English stations as well as choices between information/talk stations and just classical music stations. Unlike its television counterpart, public radio has no commercials. After that it's up to the listener. Classical, jazz, multicultural, sports, rock, pop, alternative, dance, all-news and all-talk are just some of the radio station genres available in every major city. Those stations are privately owned (many by CHUM media) and are, therefore, littered with commercials and often very repetitive in terms of music selection. For some original sound you can try a student-run station. University radio often has a greater variety of music because their mandate is to appeal to all students. Canadian content rules apply to radio as well but again, American music dominates. British music also gets its share of play, but often only the very big, mainstream names.

NIGHTLIFE

In the big cities there is plenty to do if you're looking for a little wining and dining. Restaurants offer all sorts of fare – no need to travel around the world for international cuisine. Pubs, bars, night clubs and comedy clubs usually cluster in downtown areas, but most suburbs have their own mini-selection too. Casinos are the latest rage with new ones being built left, right and centre by cash-strapped governments looking for revenue.

TAKING HOLIDAYS

Some public holidays are observed only in some provinces, but many are observed across the country. For people of religions other than Christianity, schools and employers must allow time off for religious observances that entail being at home or at a place of worship. Figure 13 gives the main holidays.

Holiday	Date	Notes
New Year's Day	1 Jan.	
Valentine's Day*	14 Feb.	
St Patrick's Day*	17 Mar.	
Good Friday	Variable (April-May)	
Easter Monday	Variable (April-May)	All provinces, but day off only for government and elementary/ secondary schools
Mother's Day	Second Sunday in May	
Victoria Day	Monday preceding 24 May	
Father's Day	Third Sunday in June	
Canada Day	1 July	
Civic Holiday	First Monday in August	Except Atlantic Provinces
Labour Day	First Monday in September	
Thanksgiving	Second Monday in October	
Halloween*	31 Oct.	
Remembrance Day	11 Nov.	All provinces, but day off only for banks and government
Christmas Day	25 Dec.	
Boxing Day	26 Dec.	

*No time off (except St Patrick's Day in Newfoundland). Celebrations only.

Fig. 13. The main public holidays.

School summer holidays are from the end of June up to and including Labour Day (first Monday in September). For universities, exam periods usually finish at the end of April so university students often have four months off, usually to work to make money for the increasing tuition costs.

VISITING FAMOUS SITES

There is so much to see in Canada, whether you are just visiting, studying or actually living in the country. It is impossible to produce an exhaustive list, but there are some things that are simply must-sees.

In the west there are the Queen Charlotte Islands, Long Beach and, of course, the Rocky Mountains. Going to Banff, Jasper and Dinosaur National Park and attending the Calgary Stampede would make the most of any trip to Alberta. You can't understand how vast and flat the prairies are without driving across them. The C.N. Tower, still the tallest free-standing building in the world, Niagara Falls, Algonquin Provincial Park and the Parliament Buildings shouldn't be missed. Historic Quebec City is itself a wonderful site, as is Montreal with its mix of French and English culture. Newfoundland has Signal Hill and a ferry to France's island of Saint Pierre and Miquelon. New Brunswick offers the world's highest tides along the Bay of Fundy. Nova Scotia has the Bluenose II, Louisbourg and Cape Breton. A visit to tiny PEI would not be complete without a visit to the setting of the book *Anne of Green Gables* or the Confederation Room. The north is a haven for outdoor enthusiasts, but there's also Dawson City with its gold rush history.

SPEAKING THE LANGUAGE

English and French are the two official languages (but many immigrants speak their mother tongue at home and with friends). British English is the basis for Canadian English and is evident in the spelling of words. It is hard to deny, however, that when spoken, Canadian English sounds much more like American English. To many it is indistinguishable but Canadians will tell you that it is only so to the untrained ear. The Canadian accent is more clipped and less drawled. Just listen for the 'ou' sound and you'll hear Canadians say 'out' and 'about' like 'oat' and 'aboat' while Americans drawl their 'ou' like an 'ow' sound.

Unlike most European countries, Canada does not have a whole host of dialects for each region. In Newfoundland, however, the accent is very distinct as is the vocabulary. The remaining Atlantic provinces have their share of inflections as do the Ottawa Valley and British Columbia. Canadians have developed their own words and Canadian dictionaries will reflect this by including the words.

If you learned French in France you will discover it is quite different from the French spoken in Canada, known as Quebecois (in Quebec) or Acadien (in New Brunswick, which is the only officially bilingual province). French Canadians will understand formal French, but you may take a little time to understand them. Many Francophones speak English as well, but in smaller towns and rural areas a majority speak French only. Federal government representatives and employees are supposed to be bilingual, although some are not.

KEEPING IN TOUCH

This chapter has been an attempt to educate on the more social aspects of Canadian life. Participating in the arts, sports or enjoying an evening out will help you meet other Canadians and feel more entrenched in a Canadian way of life. Social connections in Canada are also fostered through the telephone, much more so than in Europe and other countries because of cheap phone rates. You will most likely want to keep in touch with the people from where you came; traditional letters and mail is another method, but it is quickly being replaced by email.

Telephone

Welcome to the land of fierce long-distance rate competition. As the phone companies battle it out, the consumer benefits with lower and lower phone rates. In Canada there is a monthly fee for a basic phone line with additional charges for features like voicemail, call waiting and call display, but local calls are free – you can talk for as long as you like. Long-distance charges used to be high when there was a monopoly and Bell Canada was the only long distance provider. Now, with deregulation, you can pay as little as 5¢ a minute to the UK and 5¢ a minute for long-distance within Canada, depending on the long-distance provider you choose. A decent level of competition can be seen in the cellular phone industry. And now with the ability to make very cheap or even free international calls with Voice Over Internet Protocol (VOIP) on your computer, there is even more competition for your business than ever before.

Post and email

Canada Post is a Crown corporation and is often accused of being too expensive and inefficient, but it is reliable even if it's not too speedy. Letters within Canada can take three to five days, and overseas mail can take ten days to a couple of weeks depending on the destination. At the time of writing, a simple letter cost 52¢, $1.55 for international destinations and 93¢ to the US. Canada Post has registered mail, special delivery and courier services as well. The corporation has seen a giant loss in letter business because of email. In 2005, 61 per cent of Canadian households were connected to the Internet. Email, instant messaging and blogs have become common ways of communicating with friends, family and work colleagues. Nearly 17 million Canadians used the internet for personal, non-business reasons in 2005. Internet cafés are common in every city and most companies equip their office staff with computers with Internet access.

Glossary

Anglophone. A person whose first language is English. Geographical areas can also be referred to as Anglophone.

Backpacking. A casual form of budget travel carrying one's belongings in a backpack (also known as a knapsack or rucksack). Often involves staying in hostels, finding temporary work and frequently moving to different cities and locations.

Canuck. The informal name for a Canadian, and especially, formerly, a French Canadian.

CEGEP. A junior college a person attends in Quebec after high school and before university.

Charter of Rights and Freedoms. An act entrenched in the Canadian Constitution that guarantees certain fundamental, democratic, mobility, legal, equality and language rights to the people of Canada.

Citizenship. All persons born in Canada are Canadian citizens at birth, with a few exceptions (one being the children of diplomats). Children born abroad to Canadian citizens are also automatically Canadian citizens. Landed immigrants can become Canadian citizens through a naturalisation process. Canadian citizens have the right to vote, run for office and to enter, remain in and leave Canada at their discretion. Only Canadian citizens can carry a Canadian passport.

Classifieds. Advertisements arranged under headings, such as 'rental accommodation', 'employment' and 'for sale' in a newspaper.

College. Post-secondary education, not as advanced as university.

Common law. Often called 'judge-made law', it relies on previous decisions made by the courts, called 'precedents'. Called 'common' because it applies to everyone, this law developed in England and is used in all provinces outside Quebec.

Confederation. Refers to the birth of Canada as a country on 1 July 1867 and also used to describe the events that led to Confederation.

Email. Electronic mail, or messages sent to and from individuals with addresses on the Internet system.

ESL. English as a second language.

Federal government. The government of Canada.

Football. A game played with an oval leather ball which is thrown, carried and kicked. Canadian football varies slightly from American football in that in the Canadian game there are three 'downs' (opportunity to get a touchdown, which amounts to 6 points) while in the US there are four 'downs'.

Francophone. Someone whose first language is French. Geographical areas can also be referred to as Francophone.

French Civil Code. Civil law relies on a written code of laws. Judges study the code to find the law that applies to the case at hand. Found in most European countries, it is also the law in Quebec.

GMAT. Graduate Management Admissions Test.

Governor General of Canada. Represents the Queen in Canada's federal government.

GRE. Graduate Record Exam.

Goods and Services Tax. (GST) A 7 per cent tax on most goods and services throughout Canada.

Health card. An identification card that enables individuals to use the public health care system.

High school. Post-secondary education, to be completed before college and/or university.

House of Commons. Elected body of Members of Parliament that fulfils much the same function as the House of Commons in Britain.

Humidex. A measure that combines 'humidity' and 'index'.

Incorporated into the current air temperature (in the summer) to give a temperature reading of how hot it actually feels.

Igloo. A dome-shaped house of snow and ice.

Internet. The world-wide system of electronic communication via computer links.

Landed immigrant. A person who has been granted permanent resident status and thus entitled to work and live in Canada.

Lieutenant Governor. Each province has a lieutenant governor who is appointed by the governor-general on the advice of the prime minister to be the Queen's official representative in the province. Duties are largely ceremonial.

LSAT. Law School Admissions Test.

MCAT. Medical School Admissions Test.

Medicare. Canada's national health insurance scheme carried out by the provinces with the goal of providing everyone with a similar level of medical care, regardless of their income.

Minister's Permit. The Minister of Immigration may issue a written permit authorising any person to come into or remain in Canada under special circumstances if that person cannot do so through ordinary methods.

Multiculturalism. The federal government's policy of recognising the customs and contributions of Canada's various ethnic groups.

Province. A geographical area within Canada (there are ten) that has some degree of self-government, much like English counties.

Résumé. Another term for a CV (Curriculum Vitae).

RRSP. Registered Retirement Saving Plan.

Sales tax. A tax added to the price of goods at the time of sale. Amount varies by province.

Senate. An appointed body that provides 'sober second thought' to proposed federal legislation, similar to the British House of Lords.

Social Insurance Number (SIN). A unique personal number required to work legally in Canada.

Skilled worker. An individual with a particular set of skills such as a trade or profession.

Soccer. The North American term for European football.

Social Security. The network of government programmes aimed at protecting the living standards of Canadians during periods of illness, injury, old age and unemployment.

SWAP. Student Work Abroad Program.

Territory. There are three territories in Canada, all of which are similar to the provinces in terms of having some degree of self-governance.

Visa Officer. The immigration official who deals with individual applications.

Wind-chill factor. A measure that takes into account the amount by which the wind cools the air in the winter. The resultant temperature measures how cold it really feels outside, not simply the air temperature alone.

Work permit. A visa issued by the Canadian High Commission that allows an individual to work in Canada for a specified period of time and for a particular employer.

Further Reading

ABOUT CANADA – GENERAL

National Geographic Countries Of The World: Canada, Brian
Williams (National Geographic Adventure Press, 2007).

Canadian Global Almanac, 2005 Edition (John Wiley & Sons Ltd,
2005).

Canadians: A Portrait of a Country and Its People, Roy MacGregor
(Viking Canada, 2007).

Canada and the British World: Culture, Migration and Identity,
Phillip Buckner (UBC Press, 2006).

Culture Wise Canada: The Essential Guide to Culture, Customs &
Business Etiquette, Graeme Chesters (Survival Books, Ltd,
2007).

The 2007 Annotated Immigration and Refugee Protection Act of
Canada, Frank N. Marrocco and Henry M. Goslett (Thomson
Carswell, 2006).

Canada In Afghanistan: The War So Far, Peter Pigott (Dundurn,
2007).

Canada and the Idea of North, Sherrill E. Grace (McGill-Queen's
University Press, 2007).

Only In Canada You Say: A Treasury of Canadian Language,
Katherine Barber (Oxford University Press, 2007).

HISTORY

The Story of Canada, Janet Lunn (Key Porter, 2007).

Canada's Prime Ministers: Macdonald to Trudeau – Portraits from
the Dictionary of Canadian Biography, Réal Bélanger and
Ramsay Cook (University of Toronto Press, 2007).

The Illustrated History of Canada, Craig Brown (Key Porter Books, 2007).

A Military History of Canada: Third Edition, Desmond Morton (McClelland & Stewart, 2007).

Victory At Vimy: Canada Comes of Age, April 9–12, 1917, Ted Barris (Thomas Allen Publishers, 2007).

Canadian History for Dummies, Will Ferguson (John Wiley & Sons, 2005).

The Canadian 100: The 100 Most Influential Canadians of the 20th Century, Jack Granatstein (McArthur & Co., 1998).

The Battles of The War of 1812: Adventures in Canadian History, Pierre Berton (Fifth House Books, 2006).

Klondike: The last great gold rush 1896–1899, Pierre Berton (McClelland & Stewart, 1994).

The National Dream: The great railway 1871–1881, Pierre Berton (McClelland & Stewart, 1989).

The Last Spike: The great railway 1881–1885, Pierre Berton (McClelland & Stewart, 1992).

EMPLOYMENT

Get the Right Job Right Now: Proven Tools, Tips and Technique From Canada's Career Coach, Alan Kearns (HarperCollins Canada, 2007).

The Canadian Hidden Job Market Directory, 6th Edition: Canada's Best Directory for Finding the Unadvertised Jobs, Kevin Makra (Sentor Media Inc., 2006).

The Canadian Student and Grad Job Directory, 12th Edition: Canada's Best Directory for Getting that Vital First Job, Kevin Makra (Sentor Media Inc., 2006).

Canadian Small Business Kit for Dummies, Margaret Kerr (John Wiley & Sons, 2007).

Starting a Successful Business in Canada, Jack D. James (Self-Counsel Press, 2006).

Canadian Directory of Search Firms (Mediacorp Canada Inc., 2005).

Who's Hiring (9th Edition): Canada's 5,000 Fastest-Growing Employers (Mediacorp Canada Inc., 2006).

Be Your Own Boss: The Insider's Guide to Buying a Small Business or Franchise In Canada, Douglas Gray (McGraw-Hill Ryerson Ltd, 2002).

EDUCATION

Multicultural Education Policies in Canada and the United States, Reva Joshee and Lauri Johnson (University of British Columbia Press, 2007).

Higher Education in Canada, Charles Beach (McGill-Queen's University Press, 2005).

State Support For Religioius Education: Canada Versus the United Nations, Anne F. Bayefsky (Brill Academic Publishers, 2006).

Foundations of Early Childhood Education: Learning Environments and Childcare In Canada, Beverlie Dietze (Pearson Foundation, 2006).

FINANCE AND ECONOMY

Tax Planning for You and Your Family 2007, Paul B. Hickey and Sandra Bussey (Thomson Carswell, 2006).

Tax Tips 2007 for Canadians For Dummies, Christie Henderson, Brian Quinlan, Suzanne Schultz and Leigh Vyn (John Wiley & Sons Canada Ltd, 2006).

Labour Market Economies, Dwayne Benjamin, Morley Gunderson and Thomas Lemieux (McGraw-Hill Ryerson Ltd, 2007).

History of Canadian Business, Tom Naylor (McGill-Queen's

University Press, 2006).

History of the Canadian Economy, 4th Edition, Kenneth Norrie, Douglas Owram and J. C. Herbert Emery (Thomas Nelson, 2007).

Personal Finance for Canadians, Elliot J. Currie (Pearson Education Canada, 2007).

Personal Finance for Canadians for Dummies, Eric Tyson and Tony Martin (John Wiley & Sons, 2007).

TRAVEL/OUTDOOR

Canada Close Up: Canadian Festivals, Susan Hughes (Scholastic Canada, Ltd, 2007).

Forgotten Highways: Wilderness Journeys Down the Historic Trails of the Canadian Rockies, Nickey L. Brink (Brindle & Glass Publishing, 2007).

Rough Guide to Canada (Rough Guides, 2007).

Fodor's Nova Scotia & Atlantic Canada, 10th Edition: With New Brunswick, Prince Edward Island and Newfoundland and Labrador (Fodor's Travel Publications, 2008).

Fodor's Canada, 28th Edition (Fodor's, 2006).

Fodor's Montreal and Quebec City 2007 (Fodor's, 2007).

Lonely Planet Canada, 9th Edition (Lonely Planet Publications, 2005).

Guide to Sea Kayaking in Lakes Huron, Erie and Ontario: The Best Day Trips and Tours, Sarah Ohmann (Globe Pequot Press, 2003).

Frommer's Canada: With the best hiking & outdoor adventures, Hilary Davidson, Paul Karr and Herbert Bailey Livesey (John Wiley & Sons, 2006).

CANADIAN MAGAZINES

Canadian Business, One Mount Pleasant Rd, 11th Floor, Toronto, ON, M4Y 2Y5. Tel; (416) 764-1200. www.canadianbusiness.com

Canadian Living, 25 Sheppard Avenue West, Suite 100, North York, ON, M2N 6S7. Tel: (416) 733-7600. www.canadianliving.com

Flare Magazine, One Mount Pleasant Rd, 8th Floor, Toronto, ON, M4Y 2Y5. Tel: (416) 764-2863. www.flare.com

Maclean's, One Mount Pleasant Rd, 11th Floor, Toronto, ON, M4Y 2Y5. Tel: (416) 764-1300. www.macleans.ca

Reader's Digest Canada, 1100 René-Lévesque Blvd W., Montreal, QC, H3B 5H5. Tel: (514) 940-0751. www.readersdigest.ca

Report on Business Magazine, 444 Front Street West, Toronto, ON, M5V 2S9. Tel: (416) 585-5499. www.theglobeandmail.com/robmagazine

Toronto Life, 111 Queen Street East, Suite 320, Toronto, ON, M5C 1S2. Tel: (416) 364-4433. www.torontolife.com

The Walrus Magazine, 19 Duncan Street, Toronto, ON, M5H 3H1. Tel: (416) 971-5004. www.walrusmagazine.ca

Useful Addresses

CANADIAN CONTACTS

Government/General

Canada Revenue Agency, Public Affairs Branch, Connaught Building, 555 MacKenzie Avenue, 4th Floor, Ottawa, ON, K1A 0L5. Tel: (613) 957-3508 or 1-800-665-0354 (within Canada only). www.cra-arc.gc.ca

Transport Canada, Place de Ville, Tower C, 330 Sparks Street, Ottawa, ON, K1A 0N5. Tel: (613) 990-2309. Vehicle Importation, Tel: (613) 998-8616. www.tc.gc.ca

Canadian Food Inspection Agency (CFIA), Room 211 East, 59 Camelot Drive, Ottawa, ON, K1A 0Y9. Tel: (613) 225-2342. Animal Health Tel: (613) 225-2342. Fax: (613) 228-6631. www.inspection.gc.ca

Canadian Firearms Centre, Ottawa, ON, K1A 1M6. Email: cfc-cafc@cfc-cafc.gc.ca (Website: www.cfc-cafc.gc.ca)

Canadian Bankers Association, Box 348, Commerce Court West, 199 Bay Street, 30th Floor, Toronto, ON, M5L 1G2. Tel: (416) 362-6092. Fax: (416) 362-7705. www.cba.ca

Ombudsman for Banking Services and Investments, PO Box 896, Station Adelaide, Toronto, ON, M5C 2K3. Tel: (416) 287-2877. Fax: (416) 225-4722. Email: ombudsman@obsi.ca www.obsi.ca

Host programme 'service agencies'

Note: this is only a small selection; a full list can be found at: www.cic.gc.ca/english/newcomers/host.spo.asp

British Columbia and Manitoba have their own lists. For a full list of BC agencies go to:

www.ag.gov.bc.ca/immigration/sam/agencies.htm. For more information on Manitoba settlement go to: http://www.gov.mb.ca/labour/immigrate/settlement/firstweeks.html.

North Shore Multicultural Society (Vancouver, BC). Tel: 604 988-2931.

MOSAIC (Vancouver, BC). Tel: (604) 254-9626.

Pacific Immigrant Resources Society (Vancouver, BC). Tel: (604) 298-0747.

Calgary Catholic Immigration Centre. Tel: (403) 262-2006.

New Home Immigration & Settlement (Edmonton, AB). Tel: (780) 456-4663.

Regina Open Door Society. Tel: (306) 352-3500.

Saskatoon Open Door Society. Tel: (306) 653-4464.

International Centre of Winnipeg. Tel: (204) 943-9158.

Multicultural Council of Windsor-Essex County (Windsor, ON). Tel: (519) 255-1127.

London Cross-Cultural Learner Centre. Tel: (519) 432-1133.

Settlement & Integration Services Organization (Hamilton, ON). Tel: (905) 667-7484.

Kingston and District Immigration Services. Tel: (613) 548-3302.

Ottawa Carleton Immigrant Services Organization. Tel: (613) 725-5671.

CultureLink (Toronto, ON). Tel: (416) 588-6288.

Newcomer Information Centre, YMCA of Greater Toronto. Tel: (416) 928-6690.

Ministère des Relations avec les citoyens et de l'immigration (MRCI) (Montreal). Tel: (514) 864-9191.

Multicultural Association of Fredericton. Tel: (506) 455-7167.

PEI Association for Newcomers to Canada (Charlottetown). Tel: (902) 628-6009.

Metropolitan Immigrant Settlement Association (Halifax, NS). Tel: (902) 423-3607.

Association for New Canadians (St John's, NF). Tel: (709) 722-9680.

Housing

Canada Mortgage and Housing Corporation, 700 Montreal Road, Ottawa, ON, K1A 0P7. Tel: (613) 748-2000. Fax: (613) 748-2098. www.cmhc-schl.gc.ca

Canadian Real Estate Association, 200 Catherine St, 6th Floor, Ottawa, OK2P 2K9. Tel: (613) 237-7111. Fax: (613) 234-2567. www.crea.ca

Medical assessment information

Director, Health Programs (RNH), Citizenship and Immigration Canada, Jean Edmond Towers South, 14th Floor, 365 Laurier Avenue West, Ottawa, ON, K1A 1L1. Tel: (613) 941-5044. Fax: (613) 941-5043.

Business contacts

The Canadian Chamber of Commerce, 360 Albert Street, Suite 420, Ottawa, ON, K1R 7X7. Tel: (613) 238-4000. Fax: (613) 238-7643. www.chamber.ca

Business Development Bank of Canada, BDC Building, 5 Place Ville Marie, Suite 400, Montreal, PQ, H3B 5E7. Tel: (514) 283-5904. www.bdc.ca

Industry Canada, CD Howe Building, 235 Queen Street, Ottawa, ON, K1A 0H5. Tel: (613) 954-5031. www.ic.gc.ca

Credential assessment

Canadian Information Centre for International Credentials, 95 St Clair Avenue West, Suite 1106, Toronto, ON, M4V 1N6. Tel: (416) 962-9725. Fax: (416) 962-2800. www.cicic.ca

Foreign Credentials Referral Office, 365 Laurier Avenue West, Ottawa, ON, K1A 1L1. Email: credentials@cic.gc.ca www.credentials.gc.ca

International Credential Assessment Service of Canada, Ontario AgriCentre, 1, 100 Stone Rd West, Suite 303, Guelph, ON,

N1G 5L3. Tel: (519) 763-7282. Fax: (519) 763-6964.
Email: info@icascanada.ca www.icascanada.ca

International Qualifications Assessment Service (Alberta and
Saskatchewan), 9th Floor, 108 Street Building, 9942–108 Street,
Edmonton, AB, T5K 2J5 Tel: (780) 427-2655 Fax: (780) 422-
9734. www.advancededucation.gov.ab.ca/iqas/iqas.asp

International Credential Evaluation Service (ICES), 3700
Willingdon Avenue, Burnaby, BC, V5G 3H2. Tel: (604) 432-
8800. Email: icesinfo@bcit.ca www.bcit.ca/ices/

Academic Credentials Assessment Service (Manitoba). Manitoba
Labour and Immigration, Settlement & Labour Market Services
Branch, 5th Floor, 213 Notre Dame Avenue, Winnipeg, MB,
R3B 1N3. Tel: (204) 945-6300. Fax: (204) 948-2256. Email:
immigratemanitoba@gov.mb.ca www.immigrate.manitoba.com

World Education Services-Canada (Ontario). 45 Charles Street
East, Suite 700, Toronto, ON, M4Y 1S2. Tel: (416) 972-0070.
Fax: (416) 972-9004. Email: ontario@wes.org www.wes.org/ca/

Centre d'expertise sur les formations acquises hors du Québec
(CEFAHQ), Ministère de l'Immigration et des Communautés
culturelles (MICC), 255, boulevard Crémazie Est, 8e étage,
Montréal, QC, H2M 1M2. Tel: (514) 864-9191. Fax: (514) 873-
8701. Email: renseignements@micc.gouv.qc.ca
www.immigration-quebec.gouv.qc.ca/en/education/comparative-
evaluation/index.htm

Comparative Education Service, University of Toronto, 315 Bloor
Street West, Toronto, ON, M5S 1A3 Canada. Tel: (416) 978-
2190. Fax: (416) 978-7022.
www.adm.utoronto.ca/contactus.htm

Employment contacts

Government
Human Resources and Social Development Canada, 5th Floor,

Phase IV, 140 Promenade du Portqage, Gatineau, Québec, K1A
0J9. Tel: (819) 994-2603. Fax: (819) 953-7260. www.hrsdc.gc.ca

Agencies

Canadian Relocation Systems, 1–456 Gorge Road East, Victoria,
BC, V8T 2W4. Tel: (250) 480-5543.
E-mail: info@relocatecanada.com www.relocatecanada.com

Accu-Staff, 7755 Tecumseh Rd E., Windsor, ON, N8T 1G3.
Tel: (519) 974-8888. Fax: (519) 974-6167.
Email: www@accu-staff.com

Multec Canada Ltd, Tel: (416) 244-2402. Fax: (416) 244-6883.
www.multec.com

Robert W. Hort & Associates, Certified Placement Consultants,
225–620 Wilson Ave, Suite 230, Toronto, ON, M3K 1Z3.
Tel: (416) 636-3933. Fax: (416) 636-8113.
www.canadausemployment.com
www.canadausemployment.co.uk
www.canadausemployment.co.za

Executrade, Suite 1600, Sun Life Plaza, 144-4 Avenue SW, Calgary,
AB, T2P 3N4 Tel: (403) 252-5835. Fax: (403) 695-1795.

Attorney recruitment and placement

The Counsel Network, 1500 HSBC Building, 885 Georgia Street
West, Vancouver, BC, V6Z 1G3. Tel: (604) 643-1755. Fax: (604)
575-9156. Email: headhunt.com. **Note**: offices in Calgary and
Toronto as well.

Consultant firms

A. T. Kearney Executive Search, Box 68, Suite 2300, 20 Queen
Street West, Toronto, ON, M5H 3R3. Tel: (416) 947-1990.
Fax: (416) 947-0255. www.noinkinc.com

Education

Canadian Bureau for International Education, 220 Laurier Ave

West, Suite 1550, Ottawa, ON, K1P 5Z9. Tel: (613) 237-4820.
Fax: (613) 237-1073 www.cbie.ca/

The Canadian School Boards Association, L'Association
Canadienne des commissions/conseils scolaires, Station D PO
Box 2095, Ottawa, ON, K1P 5W31. Tel: (613) 235-3724. Fax:
(613) 238-8434. E-mail: admin@cdnsba.org www.cdnsba.org

Society for Educational Visits & Exchanges in Canada, 57 Auriga
Drive, Suite 201, Ottawa, ON, K2E 8B2. Tel: (613) 727-3832.
www.sevec.ca

British Columbia College of Teachers:
http://www.bcct.ca/default.aspx

Alberta Teachers' Association: http://www.teachers.ab.ca/

Ontario College of Teachers: http://www.oct.on.ca/

Teacher Certification information for all provinces:
http://resource.educationcanada.com/certification.html

Newspapers

National

The Globe and Mail, 444 Front Street West, Toronto, ON, M5V
2S9. www.globeandmail.com

The National Post, 300–1450 Don Mills Road, Don Mills, ON,
M3B 3R5. www.nationalpost.com

British Columbia

The Vancouver Sun, 200 Granville Street, Suite #1, Vancouver, BC,
V6C 3N3. www.canada.com/vancouversun/index.html

The Province, 200 Granville Street, Suite.#1, Vancouver BC, V6C
3N3. www.canada/theprovince/index.html

The Times Colonist, Canadian Newspapers Co. Ltd, 2621 Douglas
Street, Victoria, BC, V8T 4M2.
www.canada.com/timescolonist/index/html

Alberta

Calgary Herald, 215–16th Street S.E., P.O. Box 2400, Station M, Calgary, AB, T2P 0W8.
www.canada.com/calgaryherald/index.html

The Calgary Sun, 2615–12th Street N.E., Calgary, AB, T2E 7W9.
www.calgarysun.com

The Edmonton Sun, #250, 4990–92nd Avenue, Edmonton, AB, T6B 3A1. www.edmontonsun.com

The Edmonton Journal, 10006 – 101 Street, Edmonton, AB, T5J 0S1. www.canada.com/edmontonjournal/index.html

Saskatchewan

The Leader-Post, 1964 Park Street, Regina, SK, S4P 3G4.
www.canada.com/reginaleaderpost/index.html

Star-Phoenix, 204 5th Avenue North, Saskatoon, SK, S7K 2P1.
www.canada.com/saskatoonstarphoenix/index.html

Manitoba

Winnipeg Free Press, 1355 Mountain Avenue, Winnipeg, MB, R2X 3B6. www.winnipegfreepress.com

The Winnipeg Sun, 1700 Church Avenue, Winnipeg, MB, R2X 3A2.
www.winnipegsun.com

Ontario

The Toronto Star, 1 Yonge Street, Toronto, ON, M5E 1E6.
www.thestar.com

The Toronto Sun, 333 King Street East, Toronto, ON, M5A 3X5.
www.torontosun.com

Ottawa Sun, 6 Antares Drive, Phase III, Ottawa, ON, K2E 8A9.
www.ottawasun.com

The Ottawa Citizen, 1101 Baxter Road, Ottawa, ON, K2C 3M4.
www.canada.com/ottawacitizen/index.html

Le Droit, 222–47 Clarence Street, Ottawa, ON, K1G 3J9.

www.cyberpresse.ca/droit

Hamilton Spectator, 44 Frid Street, Hamilton, ON, L8N 3G3.
www.thespec.com

The Whig-Standard, 6 Cataraqui St, Kingston, ON, K7L 4Z7.
www.thewhig.com

The London Free Press, 369 York Street, London, ON, N6A 4G1.
www.lfpress.com

The Windsor Star, 167 Ferry Strreet, Windsor, ON, N9A 4M5.
www.canada.com/windsorstar/index.html

Quebec

The Gazette, 1010 Ste. Catherine St West, Suite 200, Montreal, PQ,
H3B 5L1. www.canada.com/montrealgazette

Le Devoir, 2050 Rue de Bleury, Montreal, PQ, H3A 3M9.
www.ledevoir.com

La Presse, 7 St-Jacob, Montreal, PQ, H2Y 1K9.
www.cyberpresse.ca/section/cpresse

Le Journal de Montreal, 4545 Frontenac, Montreal, PQ, H2H 2R7.
www.journalmtl.com

Le Journal de Quebec, 450 rue Bechard, Ville de Vanier, Quebec,
PQ, G1M 2E9. www.journaldequebec.com

Le Soleil, 410 blvd. Charest Is, CP 1547, Branch Terminus, Quebec,
PQ, G1K 7J6 Canada. www.cyberpresse.ca/section/csoleil

New Brunswick

Daily Gleaner, 12 Prospect Street, West Fredericton, NB, E3B 5A2.
www.canadaeast.com

The Telegraph-Journal, 210 Crown St, Saint John, NB, E2L 3V8.
www.canadaeast.com

The Times & Transcript, 939 Main St, Moncton, NB, E1C 1G8.
www.canadaeast.com

Newfoundland

The Evening Telegram, 1 Columbus Drive, PO Box 5970, St John's,
NF, A1C 5X7. www.thetelegram.com

Nova Scotia

The Chronicle-Herald, 1650 Argyle Street, Halifax, NS, B3J 2T2.
www.herald.ns.ca

The Daily News, 1601 Lower Water St, Halifax, NS, B3P 3J6.
www.hfxnews.com

Northwest Territories

Northern News Services Online: http://www.nnsl.com/index.php

The Yukon

The Whitehorse Star, 2149 2nd Avenue, Whitehorse, YT, Y1A 1C5.
www.whitehorsestar.com

Nunavut

Nunatsiaq News, PO Box 8, Iqaluit, Nunavut X0A 0H0.
www.nunatsiaq.com

INTERNATIONAL CONTACTS

Mailing addresses in brackets, if different from street address.

Embassies/Consulates

(For a complete list go to
http://www.dfait-maeci.gc.ca/world/embassies/menu-en.asp)

Canadian High Commission, Macdonald House, 38 Grosvenor
Street, London W1X 0AA. Tel: 0207 258 6600. Fax: 0207 258
6506. www.canada.org.uk
http://www.dfait-maeci.gc.ca/canada-europa/united_kingdom/
menu-en.asp

Consulate General of Canada, Immigration Section, Level 5, Quay West Bldg, 111 Harrington St, Sydney NSW, 2000, Australia. Tel: 61-02-9364-3000. http://geo.international.gc.ca/asia/australia/about/menu-en.asp

Consulate General of Canada, Immigration Section, Tower One, Exchange Square, 12th Floor, 8 Connaught Place Central, Hong Kong (G.P.O. Box 11142), China. Tel: 852-2847-7555.

Canadian High Commission, Immigration Section, 7/8 Shantipath, Chanakyapuri, (PO Box 5209), New Delhi, 110021 India. Tel: 91-11-4178-2000.

The Canadian Embassy, Immigration Section, 19 Dong Zhi Men Wai Dajie, Chao Yang District, Beijing, 100600 China. Tel: 86-10-6532-3536.

Canadian High Commission, Immigration Section, 1 George Street, #11-01 094145, (Robinson Road, PO Box 845, 901645) Singapore. Tel: 65-5854-5900.

The Canadian Embassy, Visa Section, 37-38 Akasaka 7-chome, Minato-ku, Tokyo, 107-8503, Japan. Tel: 81-3-5412-6200.

The Canadian Embassy, Immigration Section, Laurenzerberg 2, Vienna, 1010, Austria. Tel: 43-1-531-38-3000.

The Canadian Embassy, Immigration Section, 35 Avenue Montaigne, 75008 Paris, France. Tel: 33-1-44-43-29-00.

The Canadian Embassy, Leipziger Platz 17, 10117 Berlin. Tel: 49-30-20-312-0.

The Canadian Embassy, Immigration Section, Starokonyushenny Pereulok 23, Moscow 119002, Russia. Tel: 7-495-105-6090 or 7-495-105-6092.

The Canadian Embassy, Immigration Section, Kneza Milosa 75, 11000 Belgrade, Serbia and Montenegro. Tel: 381-11-306-3000, ext. 3341.

Consulate General of Canada, Immigration Section, 3000 HSBC Centre, 30th Floor, Buffalo, New York, 14203-2884, USA. Tel: 1-716-852-1247. (Note: also offices in Washington DC, Detroit,

New York, L.A., Seattle.)

Business contacts
Canada/UK Chamber of Commerce, 38 Grosvenor Street, London
W1K 4DP. Tel: (020) 7258-6578. www.canada-uk.org

Quebec Immigration
Bureau d'Immigration du Québec, Délégation générale du Québec
87/89, rue de la Boétie, 75008 Paris, France. Tel: 0-1-53-93-45-
45. Fax: 0-1-53-93-45-40.

Bureau d'Immigration du Québec, Délégation générale du Québec,
46 avenue des Arts, 7ᵉ étage, 1000 Bruxelles, Belgium. Tel: 32-2-
512-0036.

Police clearances
Subject Access Office, Metropolitan Police, 10 The Broadway,
London SW1H OBG, England.

FBI Criminal Justice Information Services Division, SCU, Mod
D-2, 1000 Custer Hollow Road, Clarksburg WV, 26306 USA.

Visa Clerk, Criminal Records Section, Level B3 NSW Police HQ,
1 Charles Street, Parramatta, NSW 2150, Australia.

Employment
The League for the Exchange of Commonwealth Teachers,
Commonwealth House, 7 Lion Yard, Tremadoc Road,
Clapham, London SW4 7NQ. Tel: 0870 770 2636.
www.lect.org.uk

Labor Ready, Inc. (temporary manual labour), Customer Care
Department, PO Box 2910, Tacoma, WA. Tel: (253) 383-9101.
www.laborready.com

INTERNET CONTACTS

Government of Canada	www.gc.ca
Canada Business	www.cbsc.org
Canadian Technology Human Resource Board	www.cthrb.ca
Online Job Searches	www.monster.ca
	www.workopolis.ca
Employment News	www.employmentnews.com
Society of Internet Professionals	www.sipgroup.org
Ontario Settlement Portal	www.settlement.org
Career Edge (Canada's Internship Organisation)	www.overview.careeredge.ca
Hire Immigrants	www.hireimmigrants.ca
Toronto Region Immigrant Employment Council	www.triec.ca
Citizenship and Immigration Canada	www.cic.gc.ca
Human Resources and Social Development Canada	www.hrsdc.gc.ca
	www.worksearch.gc.ca
Service Canada Job Bank	www.jobbank.gc.ca
Quebec Immigration	www.immigration-quebec.
(main site is in French, but has links	gouv.qc.ca
for both English and Spanish)	
Health Canada	www.hc-sc.gc.ca
Organization of Professional Immigration Consultants	www.opic.org
Migrate Canada	www.migratecanada.com

Provincial Governments

Alberta	www.gov.ab.ca
British Columbia	www.gov.bc.ca
Manitoba	www.gov.mb.ca
New Brunswick	www.gov.nb.ca
Newfoundland	www.gov.nf.ca
Northwest Territories	www.gov.nt.ca
Nova Scotia	www.gov.ns.ca
Nunavut	www.gov.nu.ca
Ontario	www.gov.on.ca
Prince Edward Island	www.gov.pe.ca
Quebec	www.gouv.qc.ca
Saskatchewan	www.gov.sk.ca
Yukon Territories	www.gov.yk.ca

Index